Cambridge Elements ≡

Elements in Development Economics
Series Editor-in-Chief
Kunal Sen
UNU-WIDER and University o

T0311362

KNOWLEDGE AND GLOBAL INEQUALITY SINCE 1800

Interrogating the Present as History

Dev Nathan
Southern Centre for Inequality Studies at University of the Witwatersrand, Institute for Human Development, The New School for Social Research and GenDev Centre for Research and Innovation

CAMBRIDGE
UNIVERSITY PRESS

Shaftesbury Road, Cambridge CB2 8EA, United Kingdom

One Liberty Plaza, 20th Floor, New York, NY 10006, USA

477 Williamstown Road, Port Melbourne, VIC 3207, Australia

314–321, 3rd Floor, Plot 3, Splendor Forum, Jasola District Centre, New Delhi – 110025, India

103 Penang Road, #05–06/07, Visioncrest Commercial, Singapore 238467

Cambridge University Press is part of Cambridge University Press & Assessment, a department of the University of Cambridge.

We share the University's mission to contribute to society through the pursuit of education, learning and research at the highest international levels of excellence.

www.cambridge.org
Information on this title: www.cambridge.org/9781009455176

DOI: 10.1017/9781009455183

First published 2024

A catalogue record for this publication is available from the British Library.

ISBN 978-1-009-45517-6 Hardback
ISBN 978-1-009-45514-5 Paperback
ISSN 2755-1601 (online)
ISSN 2755-1598 (print)

Knowledge and Global Inequality Since 1800

Interrogating the Present as History

Elements in Development Economics

DOI: 10.1017/9781009455183
First published online: April 2024

Dev Nathan
*Southern Centre for Inequality Studies at University of the Witwatersrand,
Institute for Human Development, The New School for Social Research and
GenDev Centre for Research and Innovation*

Author for correspondence: Dev Nathan, nathandev@hotmail.com;
nathandev@gmail.com

Abstract: The Element highlights the monopolization and exclusion from high-value knowledge in analysing divergent and, recently, partially convergent income trends across 200-odd years of the global capitalist economy. A Southern lens interrogates this history, in the process showing how developing command over knowledge creation sheds light on the middle-income trap. Overall, it shows a new way of looking at global capitalist economic history, highlighting the creation of, command over, and exclusion from knowledge. This forces us to analyse the role of the subjective or agential element in making history; a subjective element that, however, always works from within and transforms existing structures and processes. This title is also available as Open Access on Cambridge Core.

This Element also has a video abstract: www.cambridge.org/devnathan

Keywords: global inequality, exclusion, knowledge monopoly, economic history, global economic structure, middle-income trap

ISBNs: 9781009455176 (HB), 9781009455145 (PB), 9781009455183 (OC)
ISSNs: 2755-1601 (online), 2755-1598 (print)

Contents

1 Global Inequality

Introduction

Global inequality can be looked at in a number of ways (Milanovic, 2018). This Element looks at the difference in per capita income between countries as a measure of inequality. We try to explain this through the manner in which knowledge of production or technological knowledge has been created, monopolized and used in the global capitalist world from around the 1800s to the present – that is, from the Industrial Revolution till around 2020, the current age of global value chains (GVCs). This long period is itself broken down into two sub-periods: first, that of the Industrial Revolution and colonialism from 1820 to 1950; and, second, that of the post-colonial period from 1950 to the present.

The first period is that of the Great Divergence in per capita incomes between Western Europe and its Western offshoots (the USA, Canada, Australia, and New Zealand) and Asia. The second is that of the currently somewhat limited Convergence between Asia – particularly East Asia – and the West. Many terms have been used to refer to these two groups of countries – imperialist countries and colonies in the Age of Empire; First and Third Worlds after the colonies secured independence; and, nowadays, the Global North and Global South. In this Element, the terms, 'Global North' and 'Global South' will be used to refer to these two sets of countries in both the colonial and post-colonial periods.

This Element sets out to explain both the Great Divergence and Convergence in terms of a common set of factors underlying these broad trends in global inequality. The three sets of factors are (1) the difference in returns between enclosed or monopolized knowledge and knowledge in the commons; (2) the structures of the world economy created through knowledge differentiation and development policies, such as those of free trade and the Washington Consensus, which lead to adverse specialization and global inequality; and (3) the movement in development from mainly being users of knowledge to becoming creators and, in turn, enclosers of technologies with expansionist monopolies in times of transformation of the techno-economic paradigm.

The book[1] highlights the monopolization and exclusion from high-value knowledge in analysing divergent and, recently, partially convergent income trends across 200-odd years of the global capitalist economy. A Southern lens interrogates this history, in the process showing how developing command over knowledge creation sheds light on the middle-income trap. Overall, it shows a new way of looking at global capitalist economic history, highlighting the

---

[1] Thanks to one of the as-usual anonymous reviewers, whose summary of the Element's contribution I have modified here.

creation of, command over, and exclusion from knowledge. This forces us to analyse the role of the subjective or agential element in making history; a subjective element that, however, always works from within and transforms existing structures and processes.

Put briefly, my analysis of knowledge and global inequality is this: There is a process of inter-national exclusion from some critical technological knowledge, creating a resultant distinction between economies with monopolized knowledge and knowledge in the commons. There is a higher return and productivity to those who create and use monopolized knowledge when compared to those who use knowledge in the commons. In the colonial period, from around 1800 to 1950, this exclusion from monopolized knowledge of the Industrial Revolution was combined with the policy of free trade to create an adverse specialization between countries of the Global North that specialized in higher-return and higher prod-uctivity manufactures and countries of the Global South that specialized in lower-return and lower-productivity agriculture and other primary products. This adverse specialization was the base of the Great Divergence in per capita incomes between the Global North and the Global South in the colonial period.

In the post-colonial period, there is a new form of adverse specialization between the firms and countries of the Global North that specialize in the creation and monopolization of knowledge, along with carrying out pre- and post-production high-profit and high-wage tasks, while supplier countries of the Global South specialize in the low-profit and low-wage manufacturing tasks based on commod-itized knowledge. This specialization in manufacturing, however, does provide for higher incomes than specialization in agriculture and other primary production, enabling many countries of the Global South to move from low-income to middle-income status in the world economy. As firms and countries of the Global South build their technological capabilities and take on more production tasks, they are even able to move to higher-middle-income status, further reducing global inequal-ity. However, the very few countries of the Global South that have been able to become high-income countries have done this by transforming their firms and economies from being mere users of knowledge to becoming creators of monopol-ized knowledge. This transformation from being users to having command over knowledge and becoming creators of monopolizable knowledge, in an era of a change in the techno-economic paradigm, when being undertaken by large countries such as China becomes the basis for dismantling the old order and the struggle for global hegemony.

This analysis owes much to the work of Karl Marx (1848), Joseph Schumpeter (1944), V. I. Lenin (1917), Rosa Luxemburg (1951), and Joan Robinson (1933) on the nature of capitalist growth, monopolization, inter-country capitalist competition and expansion, and relations between capitalist and non-capitalist economies, and monopsony respectively; as also to contemporary economists of the long wave, Carlota Perez (2002) and Christopher Freeman (2007). The analysis of the development of the knowledge economy builds on the work of Joseph Needham (1969) and Thomas Kuhn (1962). Hajoon Chang highlighted the importance of exclusion from high-value knowledge in *Kicking Away the Ladder* (2000), while Alice Amsden (2001) showed the importance of developing the knowledge economy in the *Rise of the Rest* (2001). Isabelle Weber et al., in a recent study (2022), explain path dependence in economic growth from 1897 to 2007 through differences in the complexity of exports. Introducing the subjective element of the development and monopolization of the knowledge economy into the world systems analysis of Immanuel Wallerstein (2004) and Samir Amin (1974) brings agency into the making and changing of global economic structures. Of course, 'men make their own history, but they do not make it just as they please' (Marx, 1852).

While I give primacy to the creation and monopolization of knowledge, this is not a mono-causal analysis. Knowledge policies work in conjunction with other development policies, such as free trade, to create global inequality. At the same time, however, these development policies themselves also interact with knowledge systems to either reinforce or challenge the divisions of knowledge and labour.

How is this Element an exercise in interrogating the present as history? There is a stickiness in the history of the present. A study of 100 years of globalization pointed out that the complexity (I would add brought about by the enclosure of advanced knowledge) of a country's exports in 1897–1906 was a good predictor of the rank of that country's per capita income in 1998–2007 (Weber et al., 2022), a ranking that has only recently begun to change. In this Element, this history as the present is pushed back another hundred years and interrogated through the lens of unequal access to the use of production knowledge through the simultaneous enclosure by the Global North and exclusion of the Global South from advanced technological knowledge. This is a new way of looking at history in the present global economy. But, looking at the present as history is not carried out in order to freeze that history but to understand what is needed to overcome the unequal access to knowledge as the basis of the tenacious North–South divide of global capitalism.

Dimensions of Divergence and Convergence

The divergence and convergence are both identified as inter-country inequalities in per capita GDP or per capita income. However, underlying these differences in per capita income are changes in the structures of the global economy or changes in the relations of different parts of the global economy that first diverged and then converged, even if the latter trend is only partial and geographically limited. To identify the trends in inter-country per capita incomes and the global structures of production we utilize tables from the very useful synthesis in Nayyar (2019). While at various points Africa and Latin America are brought into the discussion, the concentration is on Asia for two reasons. First, it is in Asia that we have the steepest fall in per capita incomes relative to Europe, as seen in Table 1. Second, it is also in Asia that we find clear examples of overcoming exclusion from critical technological knowledge, as in the case of South Korea and China. Third, my own knowledge of both Africa and Latin America is too limited to be able to discuss their experiences in any depth. However, I am confident that the broad analysis of the role of exclusion from advanced technological knowledge in the creation of global inequality and the manner in which this exclusion has been overcome, through countries of the South creating advanced technological knowledge, also holds true for those regions of the Global South.

A point about the global income data – while Angus Maddison (2007) calculated the differences to decimal places, these figures should be taken as indicative. What we are concerned with are the broad differences and trajectories in the marked divergence from 1820 to 1950 and the recent post-1970 convergence, both limited and geographically diverse. We are looking for broad similarities in the trajectories of per capita income and the way knowledge is created and some excluded from its use to create global inequality, and how that has also been used by some countries to change their position in global income ranking.

The Great Divergence is the fall of per capita income in China and India as a ratio of that in Western Europe and its offshoots from 50.2 per cent and 44.6 per cent in 1820 to 7.1 per cent and 9.8 per cent in 1950, at the end of the colonial period (see Table 1). While this divergence was most marked in China and India, the rest of the Global South, Africa, and Latin America was also part of this divergence, though not quite as dramatic as in the case of Asia, including China and India.

The fall of per capita income in China and India relative to Western Europe was accompanied by a fall in the share of these countries in world manufacturing, which fell from 57.3 per cent in 1750 to 28.3 per cent in 1860 and 4 per cent in 1953. Western Europe's share of world manufacture increased dramatically from 27 per cent in 1750 to 93.5 per cent in 1953 (see Table 2). This decline of manufacturing in colonial Asia led to what has been called the Great Specialization (Findlay, 2019) – Europe and its offshoots specialized in manufacturing, while the rest of the world, including also Latin America and Africa, specialized in agriculture and production of primary raw materials.

Post-1970, there has been some convergence, though it was not quite a Great Convergence. However, as Milanovic (2023) points out, the pace of reduction

Table 1 Divergence in GDP per capita between Western Europe + Western offshoots and the rest of the world: 1820–1950.

GDP per capita ratios						
	1820	**1870**	**1900**	**1913**	**1940**	**1950**
Western Europe and Western Offshoots	100	100	100	100	100	100
Japan	56.0	36.1	37.0	34.8	53.9	30.5
Asia (of which)	48.3	26.6	19.1	16.5	14.4	10.1
China	50.2	25.9	17.1	13.8	10.5	7.1
India	44.6	26.1	18.8	16.9	12.9	9.8
Africa	35.1	24.5	18.8	16.0	15.2	14.1
Latin America	57.8	33.1	34.9	37.5	36.2	39.9

Source: Adapted from Nayyar (2019)

Table 2 Distribution of manufacturing production in the world economy: 1750–1963 (in percentages).

Year	Europe, North America, and Japan	China and India	World
1750	27.0	*57.3*	100
1800	32.3	*53.0*	100
1830	39.5	*47.4*	100
1860	63.4	*28.3*	100
1900	89.0	*7.9*	100
1913	92.5	*5.0*	100
1953	93.5	*4.0*	100
1963	91.5	*5.3*	100

Source: Nayyar (2019)

of inequality has been faster than that of the creation of inequality in the nineteenth century. East Asia, which includes China, South Korea, and Japan, increased its per capita GDP in comparison with the industrialized world from 4.3 per cent in 1970 to 21.1 per cent in 2016 (Table 3). South Asia, on the other hand, more or less stagnated in its ratio to industrialized countries' per capita GDP, being 4 per cent in 1970 and 3.9 per cent in 2016. Of course, per capita GDP did grow in South Asia in that period, but only at about the same rate as in the industrialized countries. East Asia, on the other hand, did somewhat

Table 3 Asia disaggregated by sub-regions: GDP per capita in comparison with the industrialized world: 1970–2016.

	1970	1980	1990	2000	2010	2016
GDP per capita						
as a percentage of GDP per capita in the industrialized world						
East Asia	4.3	4.2	3.7	6.2	13.1	21.1
South-East Asia	4.5	5.8	4.2	4.5	8.1	9.4
South Asia	4.0	2.7	1.8	1.6	3.1	3.9
West Asia	18.4	36.3	15.2	13.8	23.2	21.9
Asia	*5.0*	*5.7*	*3.9*	*4.7*	*9.1*	*12.3*

Source: Nayyar (2019)

converge on the industrialized countries, which would mean that its per capita GDP grew faster than in the industrialized countries.

During the Great Divergence, if the share of world manufacturing fell precipitously for Asia, in the current convergence East Asia's share of world manufactured exports grew from 13.5 per cent in 1995 to 27.5 per cent in 2016 (Table 4). Asia and developing countries also increased their shares of manufactured exports in this period.

In looking at contemporary developments, we use the World Bank's income classification of countries into low-income countries (LIC) as below per capita income of USD 1,085, lower-middle-income countries (LMIC) as between USD 1,086 and USD 4,255, upper-middle-income countries (UMIC) between USD 4,256 and USD 13,205, and high-income countries (HIC) as above USD 13,205 (World Bank, 2023). A reduction of global inequality occurs when countries move from LIC to LMIC, and even more so to UMIC status; while equality would be a move to HIC status. To mention a few countries that figure in the analysis that follows, India and Bangladesh are now or almost LMICs, while China is a UMIC, and South Korea is a HIC. They all started out at around the same level in 1950. The differences in their trajectories since then (particularly after 1970) needs to be explained.

Outline

After defining the principal characteristics of the problem of global inequality and the knowledge concepts used in its analysis, the next section deals with the Great Divergence in the colonial period – between 1820 and 1950. Section 3 deals with the post-colonial period, concentrating on the period from 1970 to the present, dealing with the ways in which inequality has been reduced, though in

Table 4 Manufactured exports in the world economy by country-groups compared with manufactured exports in Asia and its sub-regions: 1995–2016.

	1995	2000	2005	2010	2016
(in US$ billion)					
World	3.7	4.7	7.4	10.0	11.3
Industrialized Countries	2.7	3.3	4.8	5.8	6.2
Developing Countries	0.9	1.4	2.5	4.0	5.0
Asia	0.8	1.1	2.1	3.5	4.4
(as a percentage of World)					
Industrialized Countries	73.8	69.7	65.6	58.5	54.9
Developing Countries	25.3	29.3	33.2	40.3	44.0
Asia	21.5	24.2	28.5	35.5	39.2
East Asia	13.5	15.2	19.1	25.0	27.5
Southeast Asia	6.1	7.0	6.4	6.7	7.2
South Asia	0.8	0.9	1.2	1.6	1.9
West Asia	1.0	1.1	1.9	2.3	2.5

Source: Nayyar (2019)

a limited and geographically diverse manner. Section 4 deals with the middle-income trap, the ways in which some economies have overcome it, the current spread of intellectual monopoly capital and resultant conflicts over the world order. Section 5 contains a discussion of how the knowledge economy develops, ending with a brief proposal for reforming the knowledge system to undo intellectual monopoly capital.

2 Knowledge and Its Enclosure

Before analysing the interaction of knowledge and global inequality, it is necessary to set out how some terms are used, along with the framework of analysis. Knowledge, in economic analysis, is usually taken to be what Simon Kuznets called 'useful knowledge' (Kuznets, 1965: 85–7), which he termed the base of economic development. Joel Mokyr uses the distinction between propositional knowledge (the 'why') and instructional or prescriptive knowledge (the 'how') to distinguish between the former as knowledge that is used to create the latter, that is, knowledge of technology or techniques (Mokyr, 2002).

In a sense, knowledge can be called the meta-resource that is used to create technological knowledge for the use of resources. To give an example, the crude oil under the Arabian Desert was not a resource until the development of knowledge about using petroleum as fuel, along with appropriate technology, particularly the internal combustion engine. Knowledge is then what turns things into resources and, consequently, is on another level of existence compared to other resources.

While identifying knowledge as a meta-resource, it is also necessary to go beyond the notion of knowledge as restricted to Kuznets', 'useful knowledge' or some form of knowledge directly usable in economic production. Spiritual and religious knowledge also count as knowledge in many situations. Some spiritual knowledge, such as the chants or various rituals of indigenous peoples, are actually ways of memorising and transmitting practical knowledge in oral, small-scale societies, as seen in much anthropological literature and well summarized in Lynne Kelly (2015). In some societies such as those of indigenous peoples or religion-based societies such as those of Christianity, Islam, or Hinduism, spiritual or religious knowledge may also be considered superior to practical or production knowledge.

Therefore, it is necessary to have a broader definition of knowledge – something that includes not only what is useful knowledge, but also ritual, spiritual, and religious knowledge. These can also be the subject of processes of monopolization and the creation of inequality, as analysed in Nathan, Kelkar, and Govindnathan (2022). There may also be interactions among the different parts of knowledge, in both their creation and use. Propositional and prescriptive knowledge interact with each other; as do production and ritual knowledge. However, propositional and prescriptive knowledge have a different status with regard to intellectual property rights. Propositional knowledge, or the 'why' of things, does recognize the originator, but that person does not have any exclusionary right on the use of that knowledge. Prescriptive knowledge, the 'how' of things or techniques, can be patented and can thus be given some property rights (Mokyr and Voth, 2010: 38).

I have identified knowledge as a meta-resource – that is, a resource that enables the use of resources. However, once a thing has been transformed into a usable resource, that resource gets an economic existence of its own. For instance, once the Windows' monopoly of computer operating systems was established, the resulting monopoly profit became a resource by itself. In the terms used by Piketty, income earned through work can become inherited wealth (Piketty, 2013). This wealth can be used to buy access to knowledge. This is not an organic manner of acquiring knowledge but an inorganic method, through acquisition, such as that of WhatsApp or Instagram by Facebook. In an earlier age, royal courts could secure the use of various types of specialized knowledge holders, for instance, the knowledge of the Brahmins in Hindu India.

Thus, it is necessary to study the manner in which knowledge, other resources, and policies interact in the creation of inequality. This is a very brief statement of a complex issue, but obviously something that must be part of any research programme on knowledge and inequality. In contrast with the neglect of knowledge as a factor in the creation of inequality, it is the thesis of this Element that, in this interaction, knowledge, rather exclusion from knowledge, is the primary force in creating inequality, though it is not the only force.

Next, we look at the importance of knowledge in the analysis of production and then go on to see how knowledge is monopolized.

The Importance of Knowledge in Production

In looking at the role of capital accumulation and growth of labour employment in accounting for the growth of productivity in the US economy in the period 1900–1949, Robert Solow found that changes in the use of capital and labour could account for just about 12.5 per cent of the growth in per capita output; which left the remaining 87.5 per cent to be accounted for by changes in technology (Solow, 1957), which is known as the Solow residual. It is something of a misnomer to call 87.5 per cent of the increase in productivity a residual. It clearly is the major component that needs to be explained.

The Solow residual is understood to be due to changes in technology. Technology itself is the result of the application of knowledge. Looking at knowledge, or its derivative technology, as an input into production, would mean that the production function does not have just capital and labour but also knowledge as a factor of production (Arrow, 1999). Unlike the Solow model, the Romer model of growth (1990) makes technology an endogenous factor, produced within the economic system through investment in research and development (R&D). Knowledge, however, is not just endogenous in the economy, but it is also a driver of the economy.

Knowledge as technology is the multiplier in the relation between physical inputs and outputs. In the Solow model, this is labelled the effectiveness of labour, but in the Romer and other endogenous growth models, this is explicitly labelled knowledge. The growth of knowledge, in Romer's model, is based on the expenditure on research and development (R&D). This is, at best, an indicator of effort put into developing knowledge. However, both extent and effectiveness depend on various socio-economic factors, which constitute the way the knowledge economy functions and is built. This takes us to the question of why, at times, some countries can gain an advantage in the creation and deployment of knowledge in production, which will be dealt with in Section 5.

The analysis here is based on an acknowledgement of differential returns to knowledge based on a difference between knowledge that is enclosed and knowledge in the commons. This is a departure from both classical and neo-classical analyses, other than that of Schumpeter, that assume knowledge to be fully transmittable and acquirable. Alice Amsden too (2001) drops the assumption of perfectly available knowledge and technology and instead bases her analysis of development on the way knowledge is acquired and developed.

Exclusion, Enclosure, and Valuation

Knowledge is produced in various social and economic processes. Knowledge, which is the base of technology, exists in every human society, and in non-human animals, too, as the work of Jane Goodall which showed that chimpan-zees too, used and made tools (1971). Of course, there is a difference in the extent or intensity of knowledge use in various living groups.

However, in contrast to the conceit involved in declaring that the current era of IT-based technology alone is a knowledge economy, one needs to recognize that all human societies are knowledge-based and have their own ways of creating, distributing, accessing, and using knowledge. All societies have a knowledge economy, comprising 'the ensemble of its social institutions and processes producing and reproducing the knowledge at its disposal, and, in particular, the knowledge on which its reproduction as a society relies' (Renn, 2020: 7).

Looking at the nature of knowledge, it is basically non-rivalrous (Romer, 1990), or, non-subtractable (Ostrom et al., 1994), meaning that its use by one person does not reduce the knowledge of another person. This makes it a quintessential public good. The spread of knowledge should be a force for reducing inequality, as argued, for instance, by Thomas Piketty (2013). How then does knowledge become a factor for inequality, whether global, gender-based, or some other form of inequality? This becomes possible because of the other feature of knowledge – that its use is excludable, as, through social and economic processes, persons can be excluded from its use.

To reiterate, the excludability of knowledge means it can be enclosed or monopolized, as a result of which some persons or categories of persons are excluded from its use, while those using the monopolized knowledge are able to secure some social benefit, be it prestige or a higher economic return. In contrast to enclosed or monopolized knowledge, there is knowledge that remains in the commons – knowledge that can be freely used by all and does not provide either prestige or an extra economic return.

Like knowledge, data is also non-rival; but like knowledge it is also exclud-able. In an age of artificial intelligence (AI) that thrives on big data, the excludability from national data of data-rich countries such as the USA,

China, and India can also become a factor in exclusion from the development or use of technology (Rikap and Lundvall, 2021).

Differential Returns: Hierarchy of Profit Rates

Turning technology which is based on codified (and thus easily transmittable) knowledge into an exclusionary device through intellectual property laws is a widespread feature of the capitalist economy. However, it is not just the capitalist economy that practises such exclusion. As analysed in Nathan, Kelkar, and Govindnathan (2022), both indigenous societies and the Hindu caste system exclude various categories of persons, including women, from the acquisition and use of certain types of knowledge.

Exclusion from certain types of knowledge creates a social division of labour between those who use monopolized knowledge and those who use knowledge in the commons. Such a social or global division of labour does not create inequality by itself. This division of labour becomes a factor for inequality when the labour or enterprises associated with different forms of knowledge are differently valued. This may differ from one form of society to another. In capitalism, which is the focus of the analysis in this Element, valuation is based on the revenues or profits that can be earned. Monopolized knowledge allows for the appropriation (Teece, 1986) of surplus profits or rent, while knowledge in the commons provides only the cost of production, which includes normal profits. These are the two systems of valuation in a capitalist economy, whether national or global. This binary can be replaced by a continuum of degrees of monopoly and a related hierarchy of profit rates going all the way down to the normal profit of production with knowledge in the commons.

This analysis is based on the relationship between the production of goods and services and the differential economic (and other) returns on this production, which, at a basic level, must relate to the utility of consumption. To state it in a Marxist manner, use value is the necessary condition for the production, and even the existence, of exchange value. This Element does not go into this consumption or use value aspect of inequality, except to state that there are forms of hierarchal social valuations of goods and services that differ from one society to another. This analysis concentrates on how exclusion from advanced technological knowledge of production in capitalism leads to inequality.

Exclusion, as Goran Therborn (2013) points out, is a variable. There are many mechanisms of exclusion, as pointed out earlier. The mechanisms of exclusion are porous and can be, and have been, overcome by building knowledge-based technological capabilities. But, there is a discontinuity, a non-linearity in this overcoming of exclusion, based on the distinction between the use and creation of knowledge.

Adverse Specialization

Knowledge does not work only by itself, but in combination with development policies to create or eliminate global inequality. The monopolization of knowledge was carried out in one part of the world, the Global North. The term 'Global North' is used to refer to countries that were differentiated by higher per capita income from countries of the Global South from 1800 onwards. This monopolization of advanced technological knowledge was combined with the imposed development policies of free trade or non-intervention in product markets to create specialization in the world market. The first type of specialization was between manufacture in the Global North and agriculture and raw material production in the Global South, roughly from 1800 to 1950. The second type of specialization is that between headquarter firms with their specialization in the creation of technology and pre- and post-production tasks in the Global North, while supplier firms, or more accurately contract-manufacturing firms, specialize in the production tasks of manufacturing in the Global South. This is the adverse specialization that has been created in the post-colonial period, using that term solely in a chronological sense to refer to the period from the 1950s to the present.

These specializations are adverse specializations in that there is (1) an unequal distribution of gains between the two sets of countries of the Global North and Global South; (2) a difference in the structure of the workforce, and, potentially, the quality of employment in the Global South and the Global North; and (3) a division of labour in production that has become a barrier in the attempt of countries of the Global South to move from low-income to middle-income and finally high-income economies. Similarly, the gender division of labour, where men are the 'breadwinners' and women the unpaid 'homemakers', is also an adverse division of labour in that (1) it attributes household income to men, while women remain economically dependent; and (2) women's care responsibilities become a constraint in their own professional development and income-earning capabilities.

The division of labour between manufacturing and raw material–producing countries was termed the 'Great Specialization' by Robert Findlay (2019), to connect it to the 'Great Divergence' (Pomeranz, 2000) in per capita incomes between the Global North and the Global South. In this Element, this 'Specialization' has been extended from that of the colonial period to the present time. Furthermore, the term 'Great Specialization' has been altered to 'Adverse Specialization' to emphasize the restrictive development implications of specialization based on differences in the creation and use of technological knowledge.

Enclosure of Knowledge

The Industrial Revolution itself was based not just on the development of knowledge in Europe, which itself was based on borrowing from the rest of the world, but also on the subsequent enclosure of that knowledge. Enclosure is the result of exclusion, which creates two categories: whether of people or countries – those who do and who do not have access to the high-valued knowledge of the day.

'*Exclusion* means barring the advance or access of others, a divide of in-groups and out-groups' (Therborn, 2013: 59). Exclusion can occur within a country or society, as in the case of the Hindu caste society. Over here, we are concerned with inter-national exclusion, between countries of the Global North and Global South.

Intellectual property (IP) rights protection is the principal, but not the only, way in which exclusion can be achieved. Secrecy, tacit knowledge, first-mover advantage, and scale are also ways of securing exclusion. In the analysis of knowledge, there is a crucial difference between tacit and codified knowledge, first put forward by Michael Polanyi (1966). Codified knowledge is easily transmitted, and therefore, it is difficult to restrict its use, which is why copyright is critical to software monopoly. Tacit knowledge, on the other hand, is difficult to transmit and its use can be easily controlled (though the advent of artificial intelligence is said to threaten the exclusivity of various forms of tacit knowledge).

Keeping knowledge secret is an old way of realizing exclusion. However, it is also used in the contemporary world. The search algorithms of Google and Amazon, as well as the software packages of Microsoft, are all secret (Rikap and Lundvall, 2021).

These examples demonstrate private forms of exclusion. Overlaying them and supporting them are state policies of technological nationalism, which is state policy designed to prevent the export of technology through a prohibition on sales of machines and skilled workers. Britain used this early in the Industrial Revolution after it had mechanized the process of textile production (Jeremy, 1977). The USA is now using techno-nationalism to try and prevent the purchase of advanced chips made with US technology in its tech war with China (Miller, 2022). China, India, and the EU are also all using forms of techno-nationalism, whether through setting up exclusive standards or banning each other's technology, for example, India banning TikTok, as a security risk. This leads to a 'double enclosure, privatization overlaid by techno-nationalism' (Rikap and Lundvall, 2021: 20).

The Industrial Revolution and Enclosure of Technological Knowledge

Before capitalism, there were enclosures of knowledge, usually through secrecy, but these enclosures were porous and not as strict as those of the capitalist system. This led to the spread of technological knowledge along with trade.

Thus, the Silk Road was not only a trade route, but also the route through which knowledge, ideas, and gadgets moved from China to the West, usually through trade, but also through theft and reverse engineering, which often resulted in innovation (Broadberry, Frendling and Solar, 2010: 165). The later established Cotton Road enabled the West to learn much about cotton cloth manufacture through trading with Indian cotton textiles. Central to this learning is 'the accumulation – not of capital – but of experience in trading and information on commodities and consumers. This is the "Indian apprenticeship" that Europe had to complete in order to become in its own right a new centre of manufacturing and trade' (Riello, 2009: 313). Hobson (2004) points to the cosmopolitanism of the West that allowed such borrowing and integration of the newly acquired knowledge into their own knowledge systems. The weak enclosures of knowledge seem to have been mainly due to the difficulties of acquiring tacit knowledge, which is why long periods of what Riello calls the 'Indian apprenticeship' were required.

After the Industrial Revolution, the consolidation of laws about intellectual property rights prevented this free movement of technological knowledge, supported by techno-nationalist policies that would retard the export of machines and artisans. In the capitalist world economy, there is a hard enclosure, supported by the legal systems of intellectual property rights, which is now a founding principle of the contemporary organization of world trade through the World Trade Organization (WTO). In turn, the enclosure of technology, along with intellectual property rights, enables a firm to appropriate (Teece, 1986) monopoly profits or rents. This appropriation through patents can be seen in the example of James Watts' steam engine. He was able to appropriate a share of the fuel savings due to his steam engine in addition to what he earned by charging the user for the cost of the steam engine (Boldrin and Levine, 2008).

There were two stages in the development of enclosure. The first was that of the period of Empire, from approximately 1750 to 1950. At that time, intellectual property rights were quite uneven across the world. The USA, for instance, did not adhere to these rights through the nineteenth century, leading to its characterization as a 'pirate nation' in that period (Vaidhyanathan, 2017). Switzerland had no intellectual property laws till the 1950s. Therefore, there was no fixed international order in intellectual property rights of the sort that we now see in the second stage, the contemporary WTO period (also called the post-colonial period). But the colonies, of course, were not free to make their own intellectual property regimes. Now, however, there are relatively uniform intellectual property rights around the world; in fact, acceptance of the intellectual property rights embodied in the Trade-Related Intellectual Property Rights (TRIPS) is a condition for joining the WTO.

Intellectual Monopoly Capitalism

Patents form a major part of intellectual property rights, the others being copyright and brands. Patent applications require the applicant to fully state the scientific and technical basis of the product and the processes of producing it. This technical knowledge is made public, and anyone can access it. However, this knowledge cannot be used by anyone other than the patent holder, or someone licensed by the patent holder. Thus, while the knowledge in a patent remains a public good, the right to use that knowledge is turned into a private good. When we use the term 'monopolization' or 'enclosure of technological knowledge', it must be remembered that we are referring not just to the knowledge but to the use of that knowledge. In the case of patented knowledge not only is unlicensed commercial production prohibited, but even manufacturing the product to improve it can be prohibited. James Watt famously prevented others from trying to improve the steam engine, for which he had a patent (Boldrin and Levine, 2008).

This monopolization of technological knowledge allows appropriability of the additional returns (Teece, 1986) and was an institutional feature of British industrialization (Boyle, 2003). Douglass North and Robert West (1973) identified this monopolization of intellectual property as a critical factor in Britain's primacy during the Industrial Revolution. However, while North and West emphasized the incentive to earn monopoly profits provided by the enclosure, we give more importance to the role of intellectual property rights in inhibiting the spread of the Industrial Revolution to Asia and excluding Asian countries from increasing returns to scale.

Private enclosures through intellectual property rights law were reinforced by a second enclosure by the state (Rikap and Lundvall, 2021). After the inventions that mechanized textile production, the British state restricted the export of textile machinery and the emigration of artisans from the 1780s up to 1843 (Jeremy, 1977). However, the law was difficult to implement, and under pressure from British textile machinery manufacturers, who asked to be treated no differently than any other manufacturers, the law was rescinded in 1843.

The intellectual property rights of corporations have become the basis of what has been termed intellectual monopoly capitalism (Pagano, 2015). In intellectual monopoly capitalism, straightforward exclusion through patents has been buttressed through supplementary forms of exclusion. This can be illustrated by the case of pharmaceutical products. New versions of existing drugs are introduced just as patents are about to expire. This is particularly so in the case of so-called blockbuster drugs that provide massive profits. For instance, when the patent was about to expire for the dementia medicine Namenda, the company introduced a long-acting version and 'began encouraging patients and doctors to switch to the patent-protected, longer-acting version in order to undermine generic competition' (Feldman, 2018: 602). This leads to the 'ever-greening' of patents. Robin Feldman found that 78 per cent of new patents were not for new drugs but for existing ones, and that 70 per cent of 'blockbuster' drugs had their patents extended at least once.

Another method of extending patents is to enforce what is called data exclusivity. In medical patents the results of the clinical trials are part of the knowledge made public, which would mean that generic producers who can enter the market when the patent expires do not have to reproduce the clinical trials. But the US government has been successful in introducing what is called a TRIPS-plus clause of data exclusivity in post-WTO free trade agreements (Palmedo, 2021). The result is to delay the introduction of generic medicines. Overall, the ever-greening of patents and data exclusivity extend the life of patent and produce competition-free zones. 'The problem is not only pervasive and persistent, but also growing over time' (Feldman, 2018: 639). Other products and sectors are likely to have their own methods of strategic behaviour to strengthen enclosure.

Along with monopolized knowledge, there is commoditized knowledge or generalized knowledge in the commons about manufacturing or production or care work, for that matter. This production knowledge is usually widespread or easily acquired across the world, often acquired through the purchase of machinery along with learning-by-doing. This distinction between monopolized knowledge and commoditized knowledge is reflected in the structure of globalized production in global value chains (GVCs), where there is a separation between conception and execution, not at the intra-firm level, but at the inter-firm and, sometimes, even the global levels through outsourcing as offshoring.

3 Adverse Specialization and Divergence, 1820–1950

Introduction

Before the Industrial Revolution, international trade was focused on luxury commodities rather than commodities of mass consumption (Abu-Lughold, 1989). Some of them were speciality agricultural goods, such as pepper from India, nutmeg and other spices from Indonesia, pearls from Sri Lanka, and tea from China. However, manufactured goods were central to the system (ibid.: 8). Cotton fabrics from India and silk fabrics and porcelain from China were the principal manufactured goods traded internationally. Europe had little to offer in this trade besides furs and leather.

How did this global trade with Asia, the manufacturing powerhouse of that period, change into one where Asia became a supplier of raw materials and England the new centre of manufacturing? The first step was to protect manufacturing in England against competition from Indian cotton fabrics. This was followed by the subsequent mechanization of manufacturing processes in the Industrial Revolution. Having cheapened the process of production, England then propagated a policy of free trade without any tariff or other restrictions. Colonial rule imposed free trade on India, while in post–Opium War China, free trade supported economic competition from factory-made fabrics and also led to de-industrialization. India became a supplier of raw cotton, which was used to manufacture fabric in British mills.

Table 5 suggests that this was the global market structure created from 1750 to 1950, when the contribution of Asia (primarily China and India) to world manufacturing output declined from above 50 per cent to below 5 per cent. In the same period, the share of Western Europe, the USA, and Japan increased from 27 per cent to 97 per cent.

The income growth rates in Europe were not as high as initially estimated, but they were higher than before the Industrial Revolution and higher than in countries that did not go through the Industrial Revolution at that time. The difference in the comparative growth rates of Europe and the colonies (see Table 5) led to the Great Divergence. This divergence was based on the difference between returns in monopolized and commoditized market structures, yielding a divergence in per capita income.

In this section, we will discuss the role of monopolization of knowledge in (1) the global monopolization of the production of manufactures in the Global North, and (2) Asia being forced into an adverse specialization in the production of agricultural and other raw materials. This is what Robert Findlay (2019) termed the 'Great Specialization', which Amiya Bagchi had earlier called 'the

Table 5 Growth of per capita GDP in Europe
and colonies, 1820–1950.

	1820–1913	**1913–1950**
Britain	0.96	0.80
France	1.13	1.12
Italy	0.90	0.85
Netherlands	0.86	1.07
China	−0.08	−0.62
India	0.25	−0.23
Indonesia	0.42	−0.20

Source: Adapted from Maddison (2007: Table 2.22b).

imperially imposed division of labour' (Bagchi, 1976: 23), which is renamed
here as 'adverse specialization'.

There are two principal factors in the creation of this adverse specialization.
One is the creation and monopolization of the technology of mechanization, the
core of the Industrial Revolution. The other is the imposition of policies of free
trade and acceptance of intellectual property rights, which confined the colonial
and semi-colonial countries, like India and China, to the role of suppliers of
agricultural and other raw materials in international trade. We take up these two
questions in that sequence.

Exclusion from Increasing Returns to Scale

Enclosure has two effects: higher profits for monopolized technological knowledge
and restriction of the spread of the monopolized technology. Monopolized knowledge enables the person or corporation to earn a higher profit than a person or
corporation using knowledge in the commons. This is an important part of the
dynamics of capitalist development (Schumpeter, 1944). However, there is another
effect of the monopolization of knowledge which is not part of Schumpeter's
analysis. This is the restriction of the spread of monopolized technology. This
happens not only at the level of the national economy, as seen in the analysis of
Boldrin and Levine (2008), but at a global level, which is what we lay stress on in
this Element. This enclosure of high-value technological knowledge has been
a factor that has created inequality in the global capitalist economy.

The first step in the Industrial Revolution was the mechanization of production. Mechanization alone would have increased productivity, but this would be
a one-time effect. However, as Arrow (1962) has argued, there was an

additional learning by doing effect which provided increasing returns. In addition, there was also the building up of technological capability (Lall, 1992), which also led to increasing returns in a more complex way, involving solving problems and adapting technology, rather than mere repetition.

Furthermore, the Industrial Revolution was a not one-time mechanization of textile production. It created general-purpose technologies – those of mechanization, then the steam engine, and, finally, iron and steel. This set of technologies was applied in multiple sectors in a long wave of growth (Perez, 2002). Later, altogether new products were created through the chemical, electrical, and automobile industries. Capitalist competition drives the development of new areas of production, constantly revolutionizing the forces of production (Marx, 1848) that lead to sustained high growth in the capitalist countries of the Global North. Therefore, the Industrial Revolution itself was not just one event, such as the beginning of mechanized, factory production. Rather, it was a series of events, part of a process of continuously creating new knowledge to sustain growth based on increasing returns to scale.

Simultaneously, the exclusion of the then Global South (the colonized and semi-colonized countries) from mechanized large-scale factory production meant their exclusion from the growth benefits of increasing returns to scale. The incomes in countries in the Global North with a concentration of economic activities with increasing returns to scale will grow faster than in countries of the Global South with a concentration of economic activities that do not provide increasing returns to scale. This division of knowledge and denial of the benefits of increasing returns to scale, working through market-based policies of comparative advantage buttressed by a colonial-era free trade policy, could itself create adverse specialization leading to the divergence.

Increasing Returns Required Imperial Markets

The monopolization of manufacture can be seen in the cotton textile industry. Around 1820, manufacturing was concentrated in England (Riello, 2009). By the mid-nineteenth century, half of the mechanized spindles and power looms were in British factories (Broadberry, Frendling, and Solar, 2010: 176). There were increasing returns to scale in the British cotton industry, which we attribute to the externalities of learning and sharing. While output prices fell, productivity in terms of both labour and total factors increased. This increase in productivity, however, was not matched by an increase in wages. This feature of British industrialization was identified by Friedrich Engels, and has come to be known as the Engels' Pause. While wages did not increase till about 1870 (Pamuk and van Zelden, 2010: 233), per capita incomes rose steadily. Estimates used in

Robert Allen's (2007) paper showed that output per worker rose by 46 per cent between 1780 and 1840, while the real wage index rose by just 12 per cent – clear evidence for Engels' Pause (Allen, 2007). The lag in the increase in real wages only exacerbated the problem of finding markets for large-scale production. Unlike China or the Indian Mughal Empire, Britain was too small a market for the Industrial Revolution to be based on the British domestic market (O'Rourke et al., 2010). So, where does the demand that keeps accumulation going come from? Rosa Luxemburg provides an answer that links the North with the South – from the displacement of hand production in the economies of the South (1951; see also Pattnaik (1997) leading to the creation of external markets for, say, cotton fabrics. The importance of external markets was seen in increases in exports which were equivalent to 21 per cent of the increase in Britain's GDP between 1780 and 1801 (O'Rourke et al., 2010: 120).

Therefore, British innovations were largely dependent on the expansion of overseas markets. As Findlay and O'Rourke point out (as does Luxemburg's analysis implicitly), this provided an economic motivation for building an empire, as opposed to the earlier religious spread sought by the Iberian or Ottoman expansions. Britain's empire was a necessary part of its Industrial Revolution, not just in providing capital – as emphasized by Indian nationalists, such as Dadabhai Naoroji (1902) and R. C. Dutt (1901) and the West Indian nationalist Eric Williams (1944) – but also in providing a market for its manufactures.

Free Trade Policy: Creating Global Specialization

In addition, Britain did not produce any raw cotton. Initially, cotton was provided by the American South, where racism in the form of African-American slavery provided cheap labour in competition with cheap labour in the tropical countries of Asia and Latin America. After the end of slavery in the USA, Arthur Lewis argues that 'the market forces set prices ... for tropical commodities, they set prices that would just sustain indentured Indians' (Lewis, 1978: 14).

What is attributed to the market, however, is the result of a free trade policy that did not allow protection to infant industries. This policy – and not market forces alone – brought about the specialization of the Global South in agricultural raw materials. If we accept that hegemony is the power to set the rules of the game (Wallerstein, 2004), then the doctrine of free trade along with the monopolization of technological knowledge is an indicator of British hegemony in the long nineteenth century, just as the Washington Consensus is an indicator of US hegemony in the second half of the twentieth century.

The Ricardian theory of international trade, based on comparative advantage determined by relative factor proportions, justified the specialization of labour-rich India in the production of agricultural raw materials and of capital-rich Britain in manufacture. The specialization in raw materials versus manufacturing created a global production structure, where trade became an integral part of production (see also Grinin and Koratayev (2015) and, of course, Wallerstein, who held that this division of labour on a global scale was necessary for the identification of a world system). In earlier forms of production, raw materials were processed into finished products, whether it was cotton or silk fabric within the same country or even within the same region. In a sense, this great specialization is the beginning of what would later be called splintered production in global value chains (GVCs). It is interesting that this probably began with cotton textiles, where Britain developed the industry but did not produce the raw cotton. Of course, contemporary GVCs carry this splintering of production much further, with a separation even between conception-cum-design and manufacturing. Nevertheless, there is a splintering of production between raw materials and manufacturing. These early GVCs were not only in cotton and silk textiles but also in coffee, chocolate, and even edible oil, as pointed out in Tyabji (1995).

The point of an industrialization policy, however, is that it deliberately goes against market-based dictates. In colonies, the ruling power inhibited the road to industrialization by not providing protection. In fact, in India, British policy was the reverse, imposing so-called countervailing excise taxes on Indian production on the grounds that its cheap labour led to unfair competition with high-wage British manufacturing units. In other countries of the Global South, there seems to have been an acceptance of the free trade doctrine. This may have been due to the dominance of landed classes in those states, as Lewis (1978) argued. In India and China, there were substantially developed classes of merchants who could have become the class base of industrial development. However, colonialism in India and the forced opening up of China after the Opium Wars in the 1840s stalled such an industrialization policy. On the other hand, Japan's isolation during the Tokugawa period enabled it to protect and later develop its manufacturing strength, though of the handicraft variety (Morishima, 1982), before the forced opening up of Japan by the USA in 1853.

Global Monopsony Underlies the Prebisch-Singer Analysis

Adverse specialization in production manufactures versus raw materials created the condition for international trade in the colonial period. The impact of this adverse specialization on income from trade has been understood in terms of the well-known Prebisch-Singer thesis (Prebisch, 1950). The Prebisch-Singer analysis is based on the difference between monopoly markets for manufacturing and competitive markets for agricultural goods. This can also be seen as a trade between monopolized and commoditized knowledge.

The Prebisch-Singer analysis went against classical economic doctrine, which held that the benefits of technological advances in manufacturing would be distributed to consumers through higher productivity, resulting in lower prices. However, this doctrine ignores the monopolization of technological knowledge, enabling the proprietors of this knowledge, along with the colonial policy of free trade, to exclude the Global South from the benefits of increasing returns to scale.

Further, as Joan Robinson pointed out in her 1933 analysis (1933/1978), a monopoly is necessarily accompanied by a monopsony; when there are just a few sellers of cotton textiles, there would necessarily be just a few buyers of cotton. The Prebisch-Singer analysis of trade relations in this specialization between manufacturing and agricultural-producing countries did not use the concept of monopsony power. In Peter Bauer's critical study (Bauer, 1953) of the external trade of West Africa, he uses the term 'oligopoly' for a market with few buyers, what we would now call an oligopsony (Nathan, 2020); as far as this author can make out, this is because the concept of monopsony in global relations has only recently come into use, as seen in Phillips (2017), Kumar (2020), Nathan (2020, 2021), and Nathan et al. (2022).

In trade in agricultural goods, competition among small producers would have maintained cotton prices at the bare minimum, possibly the small producers' survival level, as Lewis (1978) argued. They could also go below the subsistence level as there was a surplus agricultural labour force created by the agrarian involution that followed deindustrialization. On the other hand, the prices of manufactured goods would be kept high, with cost-plus pricing providing surplus profits or rents. Even without any actual deterioration in the prices of agricultural materials, this would lead to more agricultural produce being expended to secure the same number of manufactured commodities. This is the crux of the Prebisch-Singer thesis of a secular decline in the terms of trade, referring to the rate at which agricultural products could be used to procure manufactured goods.

Like any other empirical statement, there is much debate about whether there was a deterioration of the terms of trade and, if so, what that implied. As Chakraborty and Sarkar point out in their review of the debate, 'with the development of the field of econometrics, the central thesis of the argument [over development and the distribution of gains from trade] got lost somewhere in the realm of hi-tech statistical debates' (2020: 1111). Over here, we reproduce a summary statement by Hans Singer in 2000: 'By 1938, the relative prices of primary goods had deteriorated by about 50 points, or one-third, since (the 1870s) and by about 40 points, somewhere less than 30 percent, since 1913' (quoted in Toye and Toye, 2008: 449). Of course, with short-term fluctuations and long-term trends, such statements can differ depending on the years chosen.

Enzo Grilli and Maw Cheng Yang (1988) of the World Bank published the most comprehensive analysis of terms of trade data. Deflating commodity prices by prices of manufactures, they found that from 1900 to 1986, the prices of non-fuel commodity prices fell by 0.6 per cent per year. The authors conclude that this confirms the direction, though not the magnitude, of the Prebisch-Singer analysis.

Adverse Specialization and Divergence

Did this specialization result in the divergence that saw per capita incomes in India and China fall from about 50 per cent of that of Western Europe in 1820 to just about 5 per cent in 1950? As mentioned earlier, specialization in manufacturing led to faster economic growth rates because of increasing returns to scale. On the other hand, India and other countries that specialized in producing agricultural commodities were kept away from the high-value manufacturing segments, which had economies of scale.

Further, deindustrialization results in agrarian involution or an increase in the population working in and dependent on agriculture. For instance, women of various classes and castes lost the income earned from spinning (Roy, 2020). Unaccompanied by a technological advance in agriculture, this would reduce Indian per capita income. However, another structure was working to restrain per capita income in India. While the manufacturing sector was monopolized, raw cotton was produced under competitive conditions, with millions of small-holders producing it using commoditized knowledge or knowledge in the commons.

It is necessary to switch from analysing terms of trade between commodities to analysing terms of trade between countries and assuming that one set of countries – the Global North – exports manufactured goods, and another set of countries – the Global South – exports agricultural and other primary raw commodities, that would allow a country-based analysis of the terms of trade. Given the specialization of the two parts of the global economy, one in monopolized manufacturing with increasing returns, and the other in commoditized agriculture with deteriorating terms of trade, there would be a sustained divergence in rates of growth of the two sets if countries. This would lead to an increasing divergence in per capita incomes over time. Table 5 shows the difference in growth rates in the North and South from 1820 to 1950. This difference in growth rates would have created the Great Divergence of the colonial period. This analysis is reinforced by Isabelle Weber et al.'s (2022) finding that the sophistication of a country's export composition in 1900, manufactures versus primary goods, was a good predictor of its rank in per capita income in that year. Countries that exported manufactures had uniformly higher per capita incomes than countries that exported primary goods.

A key policy conclusion from the Prebisch-Singer analysis was that countries of the Global South need to move into manufacturing to overcome the effect of deteriorating terms of trade leading to growing global inequality. We next turn to the impact of the shift to manufacturing in the post-colonial period, particularly the period from the 1970s to now.

4 Limited Convergence, 1950 to the Present

The period from 1950 to the present needs to be broken up into two sub-periods: the first from 1950 to 1970, and the second from 1970 to the present. From 1950 to 1970, there was no change in global inequality. The ratio of per capita incomes in Asia to per capita incomes in Europe and the USA remained approximately the same in 1970 compared to what it was in 1950. Though post-colonial Asia grew from 1950 to 1970 through the process of limited import substitution, its manufacturing growth was not sustained. In India, one of the Asian forerunners in this process, manufacturing faltered with the 1965 recession. Overall, in 1970, in Asia, the share of manufacturing value added (MVA) to GDP was lower than that of Africa – 10.57 per cent against 12.89 per cent (Chang and Zach, 2019: 187).

However, the situation changed after that. Between 1970 and 2015, while the world's manufacturing value added grew by 286 per cent, that of Asia grew by an astounding 3,160 per cent (ibid.: 189). The period from 1970 onwards is important because of the substantial change in global inequality, which is sharper than the rise of inequality in the colonial period (Milanovic, 2023). In East Asia and, to some extent, South-East Asia, the ratio of their per capita incomes to those in the Global North began to increase. Simultaneously, the share of manufacturing and manufacturing exports of these Asian countries also grew. Some countries also broke through the middle-income trap and moved up from middle-income to higher-income status.

In understanding these changes in global inequality, we look at the manner in which knowledge and related technological capabilities changed. First, there was Arrow's learning by doing (1962). Subsequently, Lall (1992) developed a threefold division of technological capabilities into: (1) basic technological capabilities, developed through experience-based learning or Arrow's learning-by-doing; (2) intermediate technological capabilities, which are assimilative and adaptive and involve some search-based and related forms of R&D; and (3) advanced technological capabilities, which are research-based and involve process and product design (Lall, 1992).

In terms of knowledge, basic technological capabilities are based on the *how* of knowledge, such as the way in which a machine operates. The basic technological capability does not require the knowledge of why something works. Intermediate technological capabilities go beyond the how to deal with the *why*, but in a limited way. Reverse engineering and incremental changes may be carried out – changes which would require some knowledge of why something works. Finally, advanced technological capabilities depend on knowing why and how things work. It moves from tinkering or incremental changes to the creation of something new, which involves the knowledge of why something happens and how it can be brought about. In what follows, we may refer to both knowledge and technological capabilities as belonging to elementary, intermediate, or advanced levels. We may even use the terms interchangeably, taking it for granted that each technological capability level depends on the acquisition of knowledge of that level.

To understand these in terms of knowledge and technological capabilities, we take R&D as the independent variable, signifying both national and firm strategies of developing knowledge and technological capabilities. National- and firm-level strategies with regard to developing knowledge and technological capabilities bring in the role of agency while deciding strategies. Strategies are not given; and, as we will see later, both nations and firms may or may not adopt the requisite strategies for advancing knowledge and technological capabilities. There can be vast differences in firm-level and national expenditures on R&D, resulting in differences in the adoption, absorption, and creation of knowledge and technologies.

However, before proceeding with an analysis of that period, we should point out one characteristic of the export of capital and, by extension, knowledge in the early post-colonial period. Many countries, such as China, India, and South Korea, undertook industrialization with the support of tariff protection for their industry strategies. Firms from the Global North sought to protect their markets through foreign direct investment (FDI). FDI certainly involves some knowledge transfer. When combined with local, firm-level R&D, it also involves some building of technological capabilities. However, the discriminating way in which knowledge was transferred needs to be noted.

The technologies transferred were usually older, or took place when the product had become standardized (Vernon, 1966). Paul Krugman put it such: these are old products, and 'Their technology is common property, and they can be produced in either North or in the South' (1979: 255). The North does not transfer the new products in which a monopoly is retained and monopoly profits can be earned. We see here the recurrence of the difference in returns between knowledge that is common property and knowledge that is monopolized. Obviously, a division of the world into monopolized-knowledge enterprises in the Global North and commoditized-knowledge enterprises in the Global South extends the monopoly-commoditized knowledge distinction into manufacture.

If monopolies are associated with the monopoly of intellectual property, then how does one explain the existence of monopolies based on older technologies in countries such as India in the Global South? This is the result of different forms of tariff protection, including that of so-called anti-dumping tariffs, allowed by the WTO doctrine. They are usually based on older technologies, but are protected by state action.

Development of Intellectual Monopoly Capitalism

The fact that the structure of contemporary capitalism is monopolistic in nature has been restated in the context of lead firms or headquarter companies in contemporary global value chains (GVCs) by Cedric Durand and William Milberg (2019) and Raphael Kaplinsky (2019). Uno Pagano (2015) coined the term 'intellectual monopoly capitalism' to designate the form of monopoly capitalism based on the monopolization of knowledge through IPR protection, which is the enabling condition for the creation of monopolies. The objective of such monopolies is to capture profits higher than those available in competitive conditions (Schumpeter, 1944). Such monopoly profits increase inequality in the first or monopoly phase of an innovation, which Carlota Perez called the installation period of a new general-purpose technology (Perez, 2002).

Knowledge monopolies now dominate the corporate structure. The so-called technology companies and healthcare account for eight of the world's ten largest corporations by market capitalization (PWC, 2022). There is just one energy company, the Saudi Arabian Aramco, and one finance company, Berkshire Hathaway, in the list of the top ten. At the time of writing (September 2023), Nvidia, which has an intellectual monopoly on graphic processing units (GPU), now critical in developing Artificial Intelligence (AI) systems, has become the fifth largest knowledge company, behind Apple, Microsoft, Alphabet, and Amazon.

Knowledge-intensive corporations with monopolized knowledge certainly dominate the world economy. Through offshoring of manufacturing, intellectual monopoly capitalism becomes global monopsony capitalism in its interaction with suppliers, largely from the global South (Kumar, 2020; Nathan, 2020; Nathan, 2021; and Nathan et al., 2022). Monopsony is the ability of firms to use power as buyers to reduce prices in input markets, in the same way that monopoly is the ability of firms to use power to increase prices in the output market. As pointed out by Robinson (1933), a monopoly in the product market is necessarily a monopsony in the input market. Thus, what we have is a system of monopoly-cum-monopsony in the structure of the global economy. Furthermore, there is a dual-monopsony relationship within GVCs – first, the monopsony of headquarter or lead firms as they deal with myriad suppliers, including capitalist firms and small producers who compete among themselves; and second, the monopsony relationship of these suppliers with their workforces.

The use of the term 'monopsony' to characterize contracting relations between headquarter firms and their suppliers should not be taken to imply that there is only one level of monopsonistic power in these relations. There are different degrees of monopsonistic power in these relations (Nathan, 2021), just as there are degrees of monopoly (Kalecki, 1971). Broadly, suppliers with primarily commoditized knowledge that is well distributed around the world, such as producers of garments or shoes, face a high level of monopsonistic power; electronics suppliers face a medium level of monopsonistic power; and IT service suppliers face a low level of monopsonistic power.

To sum up, global value chains and the platform economy are both forms of intellectual monopoly-monopsony capitalism that dominate the structure of global economic relations, as seen in global shares of international trade. GVCs now predominate as the channel through which the vast majority – more than 70 per cent – of global trade is conducted (OECD, 2020). Thus, it is the intellectual monopoly-monopsony structure that dominates much of international trade and global economic relations.

This is not to say that international trade determines everything about an economy and its growth. But at the level of technological capabilities, international trade is usually conducted by firms at least near the frontier of technological capabilities for a product. Production for the domestic market is often carried out with technologies of older vintage and workshop as against factory-based production. Thus, we can use the technological capabilities of the export sector, as indicative of the most technologically advanced sectors in economies of the Global South. Analyses showed that export composition by technological levels (Lall, 2000) or complexity (Hidalgo and Hausmann, 2009) could be an indicator of development levels. The trajectory of development of technological capabilities of the export sector, whether elementary, intermediate and advanced, can be taken to represent the highest technological development of an economy and, thus, also an indicator of its growth potential.

Inequality between Headquarter and Supplier Firms

The structure of world trade described in the preceding paragraph and the global economy has its consequences for the distribution of profits and incomes between headquarter firms carrying out pre- and post-production (creation, designing, branding, marketing) tasks, and supplier firms carrying out production tasks. There is a high profit and wages earned by headquarter firms with monopolized knowledge, while suppliers with commoditized knowledge only secure competitive profit and low wages as a rule.

To illustrate the inequality created by GVCs we use three sets of data – profit rates, shares of value captured in different segments, and per capita productivity in those segments.

This division of profits between headquarter and supplier firms in GVCs is illustrated in Table 6 using a few examples.

The garment brands (Ralph Lauren, Levi Strauss, Zara, and LV), electronics enterprises (Apple, Cisco, and Intel), and the consultancy leaders (IBM and Accenture) had gross profit margins ranging from 40 per cent to 60 per cent, with the exception of Accenture, which had a margin of 30 per cent. The two personal computer equipment suppliers, Dell and HP, both operate in the commoditized personal IT equipment market, and have lower margins in the low 20 per cents.

At the other end of the GVC, manufacturers or suppliers working in competitive markets with easy-to-acquire commoditized knowledge subject to the high monopsony power of headquarter firms secured far lower levels of profits. For the garment manufacturers in India, supplier margins remained in the range of 10–12 per cent (Nathan et al., 2022). In electronics manufacturing, the knowledge level required of the supplier is medium-level, higher than what is required in garment or shoe manufacturing. However, much of the knowledge in electronics assembly is codified and thus easy to acquire. Simultaneously, there is a large economy of scale in electronics manufacture, providing large units such as Hon Hai, Flex, and Jabil Circuit with some bargaining power vis-à-vis the buyers or lead firms (Raj-Reichert, 2018). Along with this, electronics suppliers are also able to diversify into other electronics value chains, such as those in aerospace. Therefore, their supply curves are not as inelastic as those of garment manufacturers. Despite that, since they depend overwhelmingly on a few large buyers, contract electronics manufacturers have low margins, at or below 5 per cent (Raj-Reichert, 2018). However, their large scale of production provides a high volume of profit, which is important for accumulation and investment in knowledge production.

In the production of IT services, the knowledge requirements are more complex than both the manufacturing types discussed earlier. Furthermore,

Table 6 Gross profit margins – headquarter and supplier firms.

Name of corporation	Gross profit margin (%)	
USA	**2009**	**2021**
Ralph Lauren	58.2	66.7
Levi Strauss	48.0	58.3
Nike	44.4	46.2
Apple	41.3	43.3
Dell	17.2 (2016)	21.4
HP	23.6	20.7
Intel	55.6	54.3
Cisco	64.4	63.1
IBM	45.7	54.4
Accenture	30.4	32.3
Europe		
Zara/Inditex		60.1
H&M		52.8
Adidas		50.2
LV		68.9 (2022)
C & A		48.13 (2022)
India		
Infosys	43.1	32.8
TCS	27 (2013)	25.9
Garment Manufacture (50 firms)		10–12 (2016–2017)
China		
Electronics – Hon Hai (Foxonn)	5%	

Source: US and European data from www.macrotrends.net/stocks/charts/LEVI/levi-strauss/gross-margin (and for each company in the table). Indian data: Infosys and TCS from: statista.com; garment manufacturers from own survey in Nathan et al. (2022), and electronics from Raj-Reichert (2018).

IT services are required in all types of economic and social activities, which means that the supply curves of suppliers can be quite elastic. Those in IT services have developed reputational assets of delivering and supporting complex IT services that increase their bargaining power. As a result, we find that Indian IT majors such as TCS and Infosys insist on, and get, margins of around 23–25 per cent. The 25–30 per cent gross profit margins of Infosys and TCS (Table 6) are at least somewhat comparable with those in the Global North.

Shares of GVC Captured in Different Segments

Profit rates only tell part of the story of global inequality. Besides profit rates one can look at shares of GVC value captured in different segments. For instance, a 2010 calculation showed Apple capturing 58.5 per cent of the value of an iPhone, Chinese factories that carried out the assembly got just 1.8 per cent, non-Chinese labour in manufacture of components 3.5 per cent, these other suppliers 14.3 per cent, and raw materials accounted for 21.9 per cent (Chan, Pun and Selden, 2016).

Unequal distribution was picturized by Stan Shih, former CEO of Acer, as a smile curve. The two high ends are the pre- and post-production tasks of design, branding and marketing that capture high shares and high profit rates. The middle portion is that of manufacture with a low share and profit rate (OECD 2017). Shares of value captured, however, need to be looked at in per capita terms – only then will they relate to inter-country income inequality on the reasonable assumption that the roles in the sectors selected represent the country's economy.

Differences in the distribution of income in typical value chains (garments, footwear, automobiles, consumer electronics, pharmaceuticals and IT services) are shown by per capita output or labour productivity from 1995 to 2015 for four countries: three of them (China, India, and South Korea) initially supplier economies in 1995 and the USA, a headquarter economy. Labour productivity in the supplier economies as a percentage of that in the headquarter economy, the USA, indicates the income difference between these economies (Table 7 based on Nathan et al., 2024).

In China in 1995 all manufacturing sectors in Table 6 were only single digit percentages of per capita output in the USA. Other than automobiles, in India per capita output was below 20 per cent that of the USA in manufacturing sectors. Korea too was in double digits, though generally percentages of US productivity were higher than in India. However, by 2015 Korea's per capita output was more than those in the USA in electronics garments and shoes. China remained in double digit percentages, though generally higher than in India. It was only in IT services that India did better than its Asian competitors, with productivity in 2015 reaching 52 per cent that of the USA.

Low productivity, or low value capture, is the norm in the South; while high productivity, or high value capture, is the norm in the South. From this value capture, however, there is a further division between profits and wages. But with low value capture we would expect low profits in the South and the opposite in the North, as seen in Table 6. Table 7 also shows the uneven development of the three originally supplier countries: China, India, and Korea. The reasons for

Table 7 Per capita real output in three Asian economies as % of USA, 1995 and 2015.

	China		India		South Korea	
	1995	**2015**	**1995**	**2015**	**1995**	**2015**
Garments	4.5	84.2	14.7	29.7	39.3	205.0
Shoes	5.0	46.5	16.8	14.0	42.4	120.0
Automobiles	3.9	14.9	1.7	4.8	14.7	18.5
Electronics	7.3	41.1	12.4	63.2	13.9	142.5
Pharmaceuticals	3.6	21.7	11.8	4.9	33.7	59.7
IT Services	53.8	20.0	25.6	52.2		13.7

Source: Nathan et al. 2024.

these differences in development outcomes will be discussed in the next section on the middle-income trap.

Monopoly Profits of Headquarter Firms Include Monopsony Extraction of Reverse Subsidies

In the previous section, we have referred to monopoly rents or excess profits. However, the realized gross profit margin of lead firms is the result of both their monopoly and monopsony positions. Monopoly power in the product market allows them to mark up product prices, while monopsony power allows them to mark down input prices, or prices of products produced by contract manufacturers in supplier countries. What are the prices lower than? We need a clear idea about the benchmark below which input prices are being pushed down.

For a firm, the costs of employing labour and using environmental services are the monetary costs incurred by it. However, the actual costs of both labour power and environmental services may be higher than these monetary costs. Using the Marxist-Keynesian notion of costs of production, the cost of producing labour power, for instance, is what is known as the living wage, varying between economies at different levels of per capita income. When the actual wages paid in global production are lower than the living wage in a supplier country, the wage difference does not disappear.

Rather, the difference between living and actual wages is extracted as a forced subsidy from the bodies of over-exploited female and male workers, from the use of women's unpaid labour in reproduction and care work, and from the rural economy from which these circular migrant workers both come periodically and then return due to illness and lay-offs (as most dramatically seen by the reverse migrations in the COVID-induced recession) and retirement. With women and other social groups (such as the former untouch-ables or Dalits of India) being more vulnerable, a higher reverse subsidy is extracted from them.

With regard to environmental services, prices for fresh water do not cover their cost of reproduction. Effluent is mainly untreated, leading to the destruc-tion of rivers, such as the Nooyal in Tiruppur and the Buriganga in Dhaka. Farmers in areas around the garment-producing areas suffer economic losses due to the reduction and pollution of ground water. Lands producing raw cotton accumulate inorganic chemicals, and the cotton-producing belt of Punjab is known as the cancer belt of the state.

All the costs mentioned so far are real costs involved in garment production in GVCs – costs that are not covered in the monetary costs taken into account in estimating the cost of garments. Given the monopsony character of these GVCs, the reduction of monetary price is captured as profits secured by the garment brands and retailers. The result is the low prices of the garment.

In Nathan et al. (2022), these unmet costs are termed reverse subsidies in the double sense that, first, they are extracted from the poorest actors in and around the value chains, the workers and the environment; and, second, through the mechanism of global monopsony, these subsidies are transferred from the point of extraction in the supplier segments of the GVCs to the brand and retailer segments of the GVCs.

These reverse subsidies are not trivial, not something we need not bother about. Various calculations show that eliminating the wage subsidy by paying workers living wages would increase retail prices by very little, for example, just 6.8 per cent for Bangladesh (Nathan et al., 2022). If we make a rough estimate of another equal increase in retail prices necessary to cover the repair of environmental damage, that would mean that an additional cost of about 15 per cent of retail prices would be needed to cover the costs of production of labour and environmental services. Or, as a rough estimate, some 30 per cent of brand profits are due to the reverse subsidy in low wages and unmet costs of environmental services.

The analysis presented in the preceding paragraph does not hold equally for all GVCs. The calculation of unmet environmental costs might be the same. However, the extent of unmet environmental costs would depend on the resource-intensity of the product. In the case of wages, an analysis of Indian firms shows that the living wage deficit is highest in the case of garments and shoes, lower in automotive products, and not present in the case of IT services, even when allowance is made for the different skill or capability levels embodied in workers (Nathan et al., 2022). What reverse subsidies do is to increase inequality in GVCs.

Knowledge and Development in GVCs

An economy can be seen as the combination of two types of firms – commoditized knowledge-based supplier firms and intellectual-monopoly headquarter firms. An economy that is primarily composed of supplier firms would be an economy with a low rate of profit and additionally the employment of primarily low-skilled and medium-skilled workers. An economy that is primarily composed of headquarter firms would be an economy with a high rate of profit and the employment of mainly medium-skilled to high-skilled workers. The structure of supplier economies would also differ with respect to the GVCs of which they are part, whether of low-knowledge garments and shoes, medium-knowledge consumer electronics, or high-knowledge IT services.

What we now need to look at is how this global structure, which is based on the division of knowledge, labour, and profits in the global production system, can develop or evolve. We look at the impact of this unequal distribution of profits within GVCs on the basis of development in both high-income headquarter economies (the Global North) and low- to middle-income supplier economies (the Global South).

Impact on Headquarter Economies

In the headquarter economies there is a fall in demand for low-skill labour, since manufacturing factories have more or less shifted to low- and middle-income countries. Unlike previous multi-national corporations' (MNCs) investments in manufacturing branches, headquarter firms in the GVC model do not need to invest in their own manufacturing facilities; they only need to invest in their own R&D, designing, branding, and marketing activities.

The resulting upward shift in profit rates and market concentration in high-income countries has been found to be accompanied by a decrease in the rates of investments, firm entry rates, and labour's share of income (Syverson, 2019). Therefore, there is both a profit glut (created by GVC outsourcing) and the use of this profit to increase shareholder value through share buybacks (Milberg and Winkler, 2013). At a political level this is likely to result in the Trump and Brexit phenomena, as headquarter economies substantially reduce the need for much of the low-skill employment in manufacturing in their home countries.

Impact on Supplier Economies

What are the possibilities for growth and development within the GVC structure of the division of knowledge and labour? Many suppliers have grown by taking on more functions. In the garment industry, suppliers take on more functions beyond the cut-make-trim of garment assembly and advance into what is known as 'full package supply', where designs provided by buyers are turned into garments. Even though the margins might not increase, the increase in the overall volume of work performed leads to an increase in the amount, if not the rate, of profit.

This participation and upward movement in GVCs has been called vertically specialized industrialization (Milberg and Winkler, 2013). It is vertically specialized in that it only targets the production segments of a product, rather than every segment involved in the creation and sale of a product. In vertically specialized industrialization, is there a linear progression, or are there discontinuities in the movement across segments? This Element argues that there is a critical discontinuity in the progress from using knowledge obtained from catch-up industrialization to creating knowledge and related technology.

What this means is that convergence becomes more difficult for economies mainly dependent on labour-intensive and resource-intensive products, for which monopsony effects are stronger. The Prebisch-Singer and Economic Commission for Latin America (ECLA) analysis (Prebisch, 1950) showed the importance of moving into manufacturing to overcome the problem of deteriorating terms of trade for agriculture and raw materials production. But the GVC advance into manufacturing through taking up labour-intensive tasks has brought about a new adverse specialization as a mechanism of inequality. This specialization increases the monopsony power of GVC lead firms of the Global North and restricts the Global South's income from manufacturing.

However, is there a way to create an oligopoly that could counter the monopsonistic or oligopsonistic power of buyers? Such a supplier's oligopoly could benefit its workers too. Large suppliers tend to have more stable order books and are thus able to better plan both their own expansion and that of their workforces, keeping more permanent workers on their rolls (Kumar, 2020). Being better suppliers, with more on-time and quality production, they could also increase their bargaining power with lead firms.

The associational power of small producers who combine could improve supply market outcomes, as was the case with coffee before the Washington Consensus liberalization (Grabs and Ponte, 2019). Product differentiation by quality could also, to some extent, counter monopsony power. Recently, Ethiopian coffee has successfully registered trademarks for its popular local varieties of Arabica coffee; and Starbucks agreed to pay a higher price for these trademarked coffees (Vaidhyanathan, 2017: 5).

The one successful case of a monopsony being challenged by sellers is that of petroleum through OPEC. The formation of this cartel of suppliers enabled West Asia to reach up to around 20 per cent of per capita GDP of the industrialized world (Nayyar, 2019). What both these examples – coffee and OPEC – show is that the states of the suppliers play an important role in countering the power of monopsonistic buyers. This remains important even in manufacturing value chains, such as garments and shoes. In China, the central and provincial governments have brought together suppliers and secured some improvement, such as secure and increased orders, and have also promoted re-splintering and relocation of units (Mei and Wang, 2016), all increasing their incomes from off-shored production.

Volume would compensate for a stable margin, but an increase in the margin is likely to occur only in the case of suppliers who have the advantage of producing complex inputs and possess what are called chokepoint technologies. Some Japanese input producers, such as the producers of small motors used in automobile windows, have a virtual monopoly, protected by intellectual property rights (OECD, 2013: 220). Even without an outright patent-protected monopoly, a complex product such as denim (in comparison to regular cotton fabric) can enable a supplier to build both volume and a reputational advantage, as is the case with the Indian company Arvind, which produces 40 per cent of the world's denim.

All these advances by suppliers, whether in producing full-package supply or developing reputational assets in the case of IT services, require investments both within the firm and by publicly funded institutes. The step-up to full-package supply also requires detailed industrial engineering. In the automotive industry, moving beyond simple assembly requires reverse engineering supported by firm-level R&D (Tyabji, 2018). To some extent, buyers or brands do help in supporting the development of technical capabilities that reduce costs, since cost reductions can be captured through lower prices of the outputs they contract. However, brands try to keep suppliers out of the key capabilities of design and, of course, branding (De Marchi, Di Maria, and Gereffi, 2018), though often unsuccessfully (Kaplinsky, 2019). Branding has now become the critical activity in products like garments and shoes. Location of production is then no longer important. As a member of the Prada high-fashion brand family said, 'Made in Italy? Who cares?' (Tokatli, 2014: 1).

Increasing the number of functions performed (and, by extension, the volume of work) is a key part of the movement from low-income to middle-income status. Prime examples of such a movement can be seen in Bangladesh and Vietnam. The Bangladesh garments industry, accounting for more than 25 per cent of the country's GNP, has increased its volume of production to become the second-largest supplier of export garments in the world after China. It has also increased the number of functions it can perform to be a capable full-package supplier. Becoming a full-package supplier requires development of managerial capabilities in supply chain management and in detailed engineering.

In the pre-WTO period, when India's patent laws only provided protection for processes and not products, Indian pharmaceutical companies developed the knowledge to reverse-engineer pharmaceuticals, creating a vast generic pharmaceutical manufacturing capacity. This gave India the title of the 'pharmacy of the developing world', as it produced and exported generic versions of life-saving AIDS drugs, and, now, it is the world's premier vaccination manufacturer during the COVID-19 pandemic, though, apart from one vaccine, the vaccines themselves were developed in the Global North.

The difference between East and South Asian development trajectories can be captured by comparing China and India (Nathan et al., 2024). Productivity per employee in garments, leather products, automobiles, electronics, and pharmaceuticals is consistently higher in China than in India over the 25-year period, 1995 to 2020 (Table 7). It is only in IT services that productivity per employee is higher in India than China. At the same time, R&D as a share of firm expenses is also consistently higher in China than India, except in pharmaceuticals, where India is known for developing generic drugs, an activity that requires a large amount of R&D.

It is only from 2015 onwards that we begin to see an increase in R&D as a percentage of firm expenses in India, though from a very low base (Nathan et al., 2024). In garments, there is an unusual increase in R&D expenditure in the last few years in India, an increase driven by recent moves by Indian garment manufacturers to move to full-package production, including providing design bouquets to the brands (Lakshmi Bhatia, Personal communication, 2023). Our conclusion from this comparison is that Chinese firms have put in much more effort in absorbing technologies and developing intermediate-level technological capabilities than India. This is what has allowed China to grow faster than India and become the factory of the world.

Therefore, development in the supplier countries is not just a matter of capital accumulation, but also technological capability development of both management and workers, which includes knowledge acquisition, through learning by doing, and carrying out firm-level R&D, with public sector support, for the acquisition of knowledge. Such movements require strong interaction between GVC supplier firms and components of what is called the National Innovation System (Pietrobelli and Rabellotti, 2011) in developing the knowledge required to advance in GVC production. In this manner, an economy that develops its capacity to not just use but also assimilate knowledge, or what Lall (1992) termed 'intermediate technological capability', could move from low-income to middle-income status.

An important part of intermediate technological capability is that of reverse engineering. This involves firm-level R&D in order to recreate or duplicate known technology either purchased or acquired through FDI. Cohen and Levinthal pointed out the importance of R&D in this process of reverse engineering, 'Economists generally think of R&D as generating one product, new information. We suggest that R&D not only generates new information, but also enhances the firm's ability to assimilate and exploit existing information' (1989: 569). Reverse engineering often results in not just copying but also incremental innovation. For instance, in the manufacture of generic drugs, Indian manufacturers have the largest number of incremental innovations registered in the USA (Mani, 2023).

This assimilation of existing information through reverse engineering and resulting in incremental innovations is an important process in spreading technological knowledge. This diffusion of new technologies is restricted by the existing patent system and often has to be carried out against the grain.

Is there, however, a linear progression from being suppliers to becoming headquarter firms and economies, carrying out reverse engineering and even incremental innovations, and moving from middle-income to high-income status? In a nutshell, developing capabilities in production or the use and assimilation of existing knowledge is relatively straightforward compared to the creation of knowledge. This results in what has come to be called the 'middle-income trap', reflecting the non-linearity of the process. For that, we must look at the middle-income trap and see how it can be overcome in catching up, in particular the discontinuity involved in building knowledge-creating capacity to overcome the middle-income trap. Before that, however, we take a look at how the knowledge-based international division of tasks affects labour.

Knowledge Inequality and Labour in Supplier Economies

The results of the knowledge-based international division of labour define or characterize the productive units in different countries. Therefore, it also affects the structure of production within which the firm-based division of labour takes place. To illustrate how this takes place, compare the structure of the workforce in the ICT sector in the USA and China (see Table 8).

The knowledge-based workforce compositions of both countries in the period 1995–2000 were virtually mirror images of each other. Taking skill levels as equal to knowledge levels, in the USA high-knowledge workers were 45 per cent of the workforce in the ICT industry, while they were only 10 per cent in China. On the other hand, low-knowledge workers constituted 45 per cent of the workforce in China, while they formed just 10 per cent of the US workforce. Why did this

Table 8 Percentage distribution of work by skill/educational categories in the USA and China, 1995–2000.

		Low-skill	**Medium-skill**	**High-skill**
All industries	USA	10	50	30
	China	65	30	5
ICT	USA	10	45	45
	China	45	46	10

Source: Estimated from figures in Degain et al., (2017: 58–59).

difference exist? We know that China mainly specialized in the assembly of ICT equipment, whether mobile phones or PCs, while the USA specialized in the pre- and post-production tasks of designing, branding, and marketing. This is reflected in the differences in workforces, with a high share of high-skill workers in the USA and of low-skill workers in China. Of course, as China has moved from only being the world's factory to creating its own intellectual monopoly-based electronics products, such as Huawei's 5G technology, the educational composition of the workforce in the ICT industry has changed in the direction of employing much more high-knowledge workers – 59 per cent in 2015 compared to 79 per cent for the USA in 2015 (Nathan et al., 2024).

How does the knowledge level of supplier firms affect employment outcomes? There have been numerous case studies of employment in supplier firms. Here, we attempt to systematize this analysis, following earlier attempts in Nathan (2016) and Nathan (2018). This systematization is based on about forty case studies of suppliers of garments, shoes, consumer electronics, automobiles, pharmaceuticals, and IT services across various Asian countries – Bangladesh, Cambodia, China, India, and Sri Lanka in Nathan, Tewari, and Sarkar (2016), and some additional Indian case studies in Nathan, Saripalle,and Gurunathan (2016).

Three indicators were looked at in employment outcomes – (i) security of employment, (ii) workers' role in shop-floor decision-making (operator system, quality circles and work teams), and (iii) wage levels. The summary of the findings from these case studies is:

(i) Firms engaged in low-knowledge level tasks in garment manufacturing and food processing have a large majority of workers with low-security employment, little involvement of workers in shop floor decision-making, and wages around the national minimum wage, which is well below living wages.

(ii) Firms engaged in medium-knowledge level tasks in automobile and electronics manufacturing have a majority of workers with moderate levels of secure employment, some involvement of workers in decision-making in quality circles (as in automobile assembly), and wages at or above living wages.

(iii) Firms engaged in high-knowledge level tasks in IT services have high levels of secure employment, high involvement of workers in production decision-making (work teams that can take non-financial production decisions), and high levels of wages.

In addition to these general employment systems, there are also women-specific systems where monopsony power is used to capitalize on the weaknesses of women in the labour market. Women in garment factories rarely last beyond the age of thirty-five in garment factories (Nathan et al., 2022); while in the IT sector, women, with the burden of domestic care work (particularly childcare), are often unable to accept promotions that require transfers (Kelkar et al., 2002). In addition, women face sexual abuse and verbal abuse as methods of supervision in garment factories (Nathan et al., 2022); or sexual harassment as a form of bullying in the IT services sector (D'Cruz, 2012).

Knowledge Levels and Labour Inequality

The analysis conducted in the previous paragraph is generalized in the 3x3 matrix in Table 9.

To this matrix, we could apply a theory. The simplest one is that the level of job quality is determined by or related to the knowledge level of the GVC task conducted by a supplier firm. This would give us the highlighted cells along the diagonal. Low-knowledge tasks lead to low-quality jobs, medium-knowledge tasks lead to medium-quality jobs, while high-knowledge or knowledge-intensive tasks lead to high-quality jobs. Therefore, the segmentation of the labour market by job quality is related to the knowledge level required of the supplier firm to perform the tasks assigned. This theory can be applied to both firms and workers in firms. Thus, medium-knowledge workers even in low-knowledge firms, for

Table 9 Knowledge level and job quality.

Knowledge level of tasks	Job quality (proxied by security) Column A	Column B	Column C
	Low Q	Medium Q	High Q
Low K	**Low K, Low Q**	Med K, Med Q	Low K, High Q
Medium K	Med K, Low Q	**Med K, Med Q**	Med K, High Q
High K	High K, Low Q	High K, Med Q	**High K, High Q**

Source: Own work, adapted from Nathan (2016).

example, sample tailors who prepare the design for assembly-line production would have better employment outcomes than low-knowledge line tailors.

However, the relationships between knowledge types and labour practices can be modified by firm strategies such as building capabilities in order to move into higher income-earning activities (Nathan, Saripalle, and Gurunathan, 2016). They are also moderated by the context within which firms function, such as national labour market regulatory institutions (including not only the state but also trade unions), and the state of the labour market. The state of the labour market includes not only matters like the overall or specific scarcity of workers but also additional social conditions such as the gender, caste or race relations within which workers exist.

Job quality in terms of security of employment and wage levels can be taken to correspond to labour inequality. The aforementioned knowledge-based theory of labour inequality may appear to be similar to the so-called human capital theory. However, the latter only deals with the characteristics of labour, focusing on whether more or less human capital is embodied in labour. The knowledge-based theory presented here combines the knowledge characteristics of labour with the knowledge level of the tasks carried out by the firm in which the labour is employed. Workers with the same knowledge endowment will get higher or lower wages depending on the knowledge level of the firm in which they are employed. Therefore, the wages of IT engineers would vary according to the knowledge level of the firms in which they were employed. Those in the high-knowledge IT industry in India would then earn a premium over IT engineers employed in low-knowledge firms, such as garment or leather products (Sarkar and Mehta, 2016). Therefore, the wages of labour depend not only on their own knowledge level but also on the knowledge level of the firm in which they are employed.

5 The Middle-Income Trap

After Gill and Kharas (2007) identified the middle-income trap, a World Bank study (Im and Rosenblatt, 2013) noted that, by 2013, some thirty countries had achieved middle-income status but had subsequently failed to advance to high-income status. Since then, other economies from the global South (or supplier economies) have also managed to reach lower middle-income status. These include Bangladesh, India, Indonesia, the Philippines, and Vietnam. Some Latin American countries achieved middle-income status earlier on, in the 1980s and 1990s. However, four important economies did move from middle-income to high-income economies. They are South Korea, Taiwan, Singapore, and Costa Rica. After that, Poland and some other East European countries also made the transition to high-income economies (World Bank, 2015).

The difficulty of moving from middle-income to high-income status can be stated thus: What happens after catch-up – after low-income countries have learned the methods of production of goods and services for the international market, and after they have assimilated these technological capabilities? How do they make the move from middle-income to high-income status?

The steps in the role of knowledge in the development from low- to middle-income and then to high-income economies are schematically summarized in Table 10.

This figure can be applied both at the GVC and national per-capita-GDP levels. An economy that is basically in assembly (and the production of agricultural raw materials) will be a low-income economy. An economy that takes up full-package supply, which means it also includes assembly, will be a medium-income economy, while an economy specializing in design, branding, and marketing activities will be a high-income economy. In each step of evolution, the knowledge content of economic activity increases. A somewhat similar scheme of movement through GVCs, where the knowledge content (or disembodied content, as they term it) increases, is found in Kaplinsky and Morris (2001).

Milberg and Winkler (2013) find some evidence for this schematic analysis. They plot vertical specialization against per capita GDP and find that LICs are specialized in the same way as HICs. The two exist in opposite ends of the GVC spectrum – the LICs in assembly and the HICs in design, branding and marketing. It is the MICs that are least specialized: 'low-income countries seek to upgrade by reducing the overall level of vertical specialization (raising domestic value added in exports) and then reaching a point where rising incomes involves increased vertical specialization while focusing on the

Table 10 Knowledge, profits, and development.

	Profits and per capita GDP		
Knowledge bases of production segments	Low	Medium	High
Low	Assembly		
Medium		Full-package supply	
High			Design/Brand/Market

Source: Adapted from Nathan (2018)

highest value-added component of the GVC' (Milberg and Winkler, 2013: 308–9). I would amend 'value added component' to 'value capturing component', which brings the elements of monopoly and monopsony power into the analysis of the distribution of value within a GVC.

The difference between lead and supplier firms in the production of goods and the monopolization of profits by the former are clear. So is the role of own-brand GVCs in the movement towards high-income status. However, knowledge-intensive services can also play a role in this movement out of the middle-income stage, as seen in Singapore, Taiwan, Hong Kong and, more recently, Poland (World Bank, 2015).

In the matter of services, the differentiation is between companies (for example, IT services) that provide end-to-end services, including high-end consulting and programming, testing and maintenance, and those who provide mainly the latter set of programming, testing and maintenance. This leads to very large differences in revenue per employee – $193,395 and $116,729 for IBM and Accenture respectively in 2021, compared to $55,229 and $45,300 for the Indian IT service majors Infosys and TCS respectively (all data from www.statista.com, 2022). A movement to high-value end-to-end consulting needs to replace the performance of subsidiary functions in order to support the movement from middle-income to high-income status.

The important implication of our analysis is that in order to make the transition from middle-income to high-income status, the critical factor is the development of knowledge, as also argued by Kuen Lee (2013). To his analysis, we add that what is required is knowledge which can be monopolized through intellectual property rights and become the basis of both headquarter lead firms and high-value services. From being users of knowledge, supplier economies must become creators of knowledge. This has been accomplished by very few countries – one is South Korea. China is certainly moving in that direction as it develops its knowledge economy.

What is involved may not be just a general advance in knowledge creation, but something targeted at frontier technologies. Lee's Schumpeterian analysis of movement to high-income status points out that Korea and Taiwan were able to advance in 'short-cycle' frontier technologies such as consumer electronics and chip-making, where the capabilities required were different from and subject to less competition than in the older technologies (Lee, 2013).

China has taken up a different strategy of developing not just 'short-cycle' technologies, but of advancing in the new general-purpose technologies of Artificial Intelligence (AI) and quantum computing. This is the time of a change in the techno-economic paradigm (Perez, 2002), and it provides opportunities for newcomers to challenge the established hegemons

(Freeman, 2007). In new technologies, technological capabilities, such as in AI today, are not well developed in any country – not only those of the Global South but even those of the Global North. This makes it possible for an emerging economy to develop as a world-class leader in, say, artificial intelligence, electric mobility, renewable energy, or drones.

The USA supplanted Britain in the transition from iron and steel to oil, automobiles, and electricity (Perez, 2002: 11). In a similar fashion, a large economy such as China may try to leap-frog in the development of the new general-purpose technology to push for a change in the economic order. It is China's strategy to be the world leader in AI by 2030 (Suleyman, 2023). India too is making its push in AI, though as the official economic policy think-tank admits, 'India sees itself lagging considerably behind in producing world-class research in most technology fields, more so in AI' (Niti Aayog 2020: 50).

Thus, moving out of the middle-income traps requires a change in the existing broad division of labour in the global knowledge economy, between the new product-developing monopolies of the Global North and manufacturing suppliers of the Global South; which itself requires a movement from being users of knowledge as manufacturing suppliers to becoming producers of knowledge. This requires not just an increase in the supply of highly educated workers but also in the demand for such highly educated workers (Arocena and Sutz, 2010). Increased supply with weak domestic demand for high-knowledge workers is seen quite starkly in the case of India, which supplies not just large numbers of high-knowledge workers to the global economy, but even CEOs of major US IT corporations like Microsoft and Google, while itself having a low demand for these knowledge creators.

The demand for highly educated workers to create knowledge can be illustrated with a key indicator, that of expenditure on R&D as a proportion of GDP, which acts as a proxy indicator for the demand for knowledge creation. Table 11 shows the clear divide between low-income, middle-income, and high-income countries.

What this table notes is formal R&D expenditure. It does not include the countless knowledge creations and innovations, which are mainly carried out in improving production processes. These are of the type called *jugaad* in India and are of the tinkering variety. They do not fall into the category of knowledge that can be monopolized or provide excess profits. R&D expenditure is a rough indicator of the size of a country's overall scientific and innovation establishments, which themselves are part of the overall knowledge economy embedded in the socio-economic system. What remains to be analysed in the next step is 'how some actors in the global economy manage to "enclose" high-value technological knowledge' (Appadurai, 2022). The monopolization of

Table 11 R&D expenditures by country groups.

Economy Group/ country (1)	R&D Expenditures as % of GDP 2010–2018 (2)	R&D Expenditures as % of GDP 2020 (3)
Low income	-	-
Lower middle income	0.58	
Upper middle income	1.75	1.65
High income	2.59	2.95
India	0.65	0.65
Brazil	1.26	1.15
South Africa	0.83	0.60
China	2.19	2.41
Korea	4.81	4.80
USA	2.84	3.47
Germany	3.09	3.13
Japan	3.26	3.27

Source: World Development Indicators, 2020, Science and Technology, http://wdi.worldbank.org/table/5.13 and UNESCO, 2023,

knowledge through intellectual property rights, as seen in Section 2, is the instrument for such enclosure. The processes that lead to the creation of knowledge leading to enclosure in a globally connected economy need to be identified. This is taken up in the next section.

Expenditure on R&D is for the absorption and creation of new knowledge, whether incremental or more basic. There is a correspondence between R&D expenditure as a percentage of GDP and income status in Table 11; but this is a two-way relationship. Increasing R&D expenditure is necessary for increasing income status, particularly for low- or middle-income countries; at the same time, income status also affects the ability to devote expenditure to R&D. China, with an R&D-to-GDP ratio of 2.19 per cent, which is higher than the average for upper-middle-income countries and close to the average of 2.59 per cent for high-income countries, exhibits a clear policy of moving from knowledge utilization to knowledge creation – just as Korea, Singapore, and Taiwan did earlier. Brazil, India, and South Africa, on the other hand, are all lagging in investment in knowledge creation.

However, things are changing there as well, as shown by the creation of COVID-19 vaccines in both India and South Africa, apart from China. In electric vehicles, the Chinese manufacturer BYD has built its own battery and related technologies, an area dominated by the Japanese as recently as 2006 (Yuan and Li, 2021). The advance of China on a broad front is reflected in the number of patents granted in the stringent US Patent Office to Chinese entities – the number went up from 256 in 2001 to nearly 20,000 in 2021, overtaking Germany's 19,000 in 2021 (Oughton and Tobin, 2023). India does not show comparable advances in the private sector, but has advanced in creating hyper-scale public digital infrastructure, as in biometric identification and payment systems.

The global order in new applications of knowledge is captured in the Global Innovation Index (GII) crafted by the World Intellectual Property Organization (WIPO). The GII bears out the changes that are underway (WIPO, 2021). China ranks 12th overall and 1st in the upper-middle-income group. India ranks 40th overall and 2nd in the lower-middle-income group, where even Vietnam ranks above India (WIPO, 2021: 4).

At the regional level, the WIPO report points out that Southeast Asia, East Asia, and Oceania are the only regions that are closing the gap with North America and Europe in the GII. WIPO points out that the innovation landscape is changing in middle-income countries, with China, Turkey, Vietnam, India, and the Philippines advancing in the innovation landscape in that order. On the other hand, Latin America does particularly poorly, with only Mexico having consistently increased its ranking over the past ten years. This picture is what we would expect given the relatively long stagnation of Latin America in the middle-income trap, while East Asia is catching up with North America and Europe. At the same time, a few other middle-income countries like Turkey, Vietnam, India, and the Philippines are also moving ahead.

An analysis of innovation in five Latin American economies (Paus and Robinson, 2022) shows that firm-level R&D investment in China is more likely to result in a new product than in the Latin American economies studied. They attribute this weakness to the differences in the respective national innovation systems, including stronger state support in China. That is correct, but only part of the answer. Our analysis would suggest that Latin American firms and states have concentrated on incremental innovations and not on the creation of knowledge for new products and brands with patents, as mentioned earlier. China has adopted a clear strategy, as did Korea earlier, of being at the technological frontier and developing new products and their own brands.

From Nationalism to Expansionism

Moving into knowledge creation and using that to develop enterprises will inevitably mean competition for markets between old incumbents and newcomers. In these struggles for dominance (such as in the sphere of platforms), the big players headquartered in India or China have received direct or indirect support from their respective states. When Uber sold out to the Chinese taxi service Didi Chuxing, the sale was reported to be orchestrated by the Chinese government (Jannace and Tiffany, 2019).

This has been objected to as techno-nationalism and a movement from the rule of law to that of rulers (Jannace and Tiffany, 2019). Of course, the law here is TRIPS, which is part of the WTO's articles of membership. However, techno-nationalism, defined as 'government action in support of high-tech industries' (Ostry and Nelson, 1995: 61), is not something new. The US state played a role in the rise of American technological leadership – shown in detail by Marianna Mazzucatto (2013) and continues to be part of American policy. The EU's 'Europe First Policy' (Ernst, 2012) is a form of techno-nationalism, where the relevant geography has been extended from relatively small European nations to the European Union in order to be able to utilize economies of scale, which are important in platform economics.

Techno-nationalism has been part of development policy for late-comers, while technology leaders have tried to stop this by insisting on the adoption of market-fundamentalist policies by developing countries and the abandonment of nation-based technology policies, which Ha Joon Chang picturesquely characterized as 'Kicking away the ladder [after having ascended it]' (Chang, 2000). For instance, in order to catch up, the USA did not enforce British or German patents or copyright in the nineteenth century, leading to the characterization of nineteenth-century USA as a 'pirate nation' (Vaidhyanathan, 2017: 13). Later, as US firms developed their own technologies, the USA started insisting on the strict application of patent laws. Non-acceptance of patents by low- and middle-income countries is no longer possible, though, as acceptance of IPR protection under TRIPS is a condition of being a member of the WTO. Nevertheless, states have continued to find ways around TRIPS regulations.

For instance, China, has erected substantial barriers for non-Chinese platforms in digital trade. The story of keeping Google or Amazon out of China so that Baidu (a search engine) and Alibaba (an e-commerce portal) could develop is well known. However, it is not just China that is taking such nationalist actions. The USA, the EU, and China have all taken steps leading to the evolution of separate digital regimes that are not necessarily compatible. Now, India, Russia, Vietnam, and Indonesia are building their own digital regimes. The USA is trying to prevent China from acquiring the most critical chip technologies.

There are two points about techno-nationalism. First, it is an inevitable part of development policy, as late-comers try to catch up with tech leaders. Such catching up cannot be accomplished or even attempted in the absence of a close relationship between the state, firms, and technology policy (Mazzucato, 2013). Second, in a capitalist world economy, such catching-up is a prelude to expansionism. Capital will seek to expand and must necessarily cross national borders; the intellectual monopoly capitalism of headquarter firms in both established and emerging headquarter economies reinforces this expansionist feature. Thus, monopoly capitalism is necessarily expansionist in its search for markets, which leads to inter-country competition for spheres of influence (Lenin, 1917). It is the development of the knowledge economy that enables the creation of new, emerging, headquarter economies and their expansionist moves that combine economic power with political, military, and even soft cultural power.

Therefore, after securing its own national technological platforms, China is now attempting to expand its role and influence in the world economy. Its own digital technology leadership in 5G mobile technology, which has brought it into conflict with the USA, is now being used to build what the Chinese call the Digital Silk Road.

India has also been moving on the road of digital techno-nationalism. Many actions have been taken against Chinese companies in India, including the banning of TikTok. Ola, the Indian taxi platform, and OYO, the Indian hotel platform, have both expanded into other countries. Therefore, they have become regional firms, if not global ones. Of course, many of the established Indian conglomerate-headquarter firms, such as Reliance, Adani, Tata and Mahindra, the IT majors, TCS, Infosys, Wipro, and the major pharmaceutical manufacturers, are already global players.

In this movement from nationalism to expansion, the new players also combine monopoly with monopsony. Leading firms set up their own zones of monopsony and compete with each other, as is clearly visible across Africa and Latin America, with a scramble for the newly critical natural resources, such as lithium and cobalt (Kepe et al., 2023). In this development, it is not possible to draw a Chinese wall to separate nationalism from expansionism – even more so when there are monopolies. Also, in a capitalist system, it is inevitable that expansionism in seeking advantages in markets will follow successful tech nationalism. This is particularly so when new types of platform-based hyper-enterprises are created, which have the enormous advantages of hyper-scale and can easily be built to scale simultaneously in numerous countries.

Such expansionism and the defence of entrenched positions have become part of the geo-strategic struggle to redraw the contours of the world. The monopolization of knowledge itself is part of the geo-political struggle, as the USA tries to prevent China from catching-up in high-tech chip design and manufacture, while China invests to build a lead in AI and quantum computing as the next-generation general-purpose technologies.

Interdependencies that are characteristic of GVC organization are being weaponized (Drezner, Farrell and Newman, 2021). GVCs are also being recreated in this context. An example is the movement out of China, which is not only a reaction to higher wages in China, but also stems from the USA and other countries' strategy of reducing reliance on China. Given the cost-effectiveness of off-shoring to low-wage areas, the value chain movement is unlikely to result in onshoring within the USA, but more likely to cause what Janet Yellen, the US Secretary of the Treasury, called 'friend-shoring'. This has been accompanied by a renewed US emphasis on Latin America, whose reserve of surplus labour could replace some of the US value chains that are now linked to China.

Multipolar jostling surrounds the main conflict between the USA and China, but the EU and India are also part of the mix. The multipolar globalization that is now visibly growing will not result in the end of conflicts; instead, it will only intensify geo-strategic conflicts as each new pole jostles with older poles to try to make its own space in areas now under the control of others.

Monopolized knowledge is power. But advanced technical knowledge has to be developed in order for it to be monopolized. So far we have dealt with knowledge as being created by investment in R&D. This is a practice that is relatively easy to copy. But expenditure on R&D is just short form for what is really a complex process of development of the knowledge economy. This is dealt with in the next section moving from an economic to a sociological analysis of factors that influence the development of the knowledge economy.

6 Building the Knowledge Economy

Overcoming the middle-income trap requires moving from the use of knowledge, including its deployment in incremental innovations to the creation of knowledge and products or services based on them. So far the only factor we have considered for the creation of knowledge is that of investment in R&D. That is important as an indicator, whether at the country or firm level. But the creation of knowledge is much more than just that. It involves dealing with both the sociology, or *how*, of knowledge and its political economy, or *why*, of knowledge creation. For instance, R&D or investment in science and technology (S&T) is a critical input in the development of technological knowledge, but why do some countries and firms place more stress on this than other countries and firms? Why did India invest 0.65 per cent, China 2.41 per cent, and Korea 4.80 per cent of GDP in R&D in 2020 (Table 11). This is a difficult question to answer. It is, as Mark Taylor (2016) points out, the why of S&T or knowledge development. How effective this expenditure on R&D is depends on the institutions and incentives for knowledge development, the how of knowledge development. This section deals with these two questions, the why and how of knowledge development, in that order.

Explanations of Divergence in Knowledge

Economic historians have generally accepted that the Great Divergence between the West and East (or Global North and Global South, as we have renamed them here) was due to the divergence in knowledge in production between these two sets of countries. However, there is much debate about why and how this divergence in knowledge came about. Joseph Needham, a historian of Chinese science and technology, who was well aware of Chinese scientific advances before Western dominance, posed the question of the divergence in a comparative and counter-factual manner, 'Why did the Scientific Revolution take place in the West and not in China (or India)?'[2] This question seeks to identify what was lacking in the East that was present in the West, which is a decidedly one-sided comparison, taking the European as the standard to be emulated.

In an email exchange with this Element's author on the topic of knowledge and global inequality, Arjun Appadurai pointed out the need to analyse 'how some actors in the global economy manage to "enclose" high-value technological knowledge' (Appadurai, 2022). This is not a Eurocentric formulation, as it does not just deal with the scientific revolution that led to the Industrial Revolution but deals more generally with leadership in and enclosure of technological knowledge. Jack Goody (1996), John Hobson (2004), and Jurgen Renn (2020) all take up non-Eurocentric formulations of the evolution of knowledge.

What could constitute the components of an answer to the question: why can some actors/powers in the global economy develop and monopolize high-valued technological knowledge? There have been several approaches to answering this question, even if the question was not posed in the manner mentioned here.

The first set of answers is related to the developments in Western European countries that led to changes in their structures and to a demand for technological advances. Marx found this in the development of capitalism, where competition drove the constant revolutionizing of the means of production (1848). Marx's analysis was modified by Joseph Schumpeter (1944), who

---

[2] There are many versions of this question. See Needham (1969).

pointed to the monopoly profits of new technology as the driver of 'creative destruction' in the revolutionizing of technology.

A different type of answer was put forward by those who are identified as the California School, who gave primacy to contingency. Contingency relates to the resources and problems that were being faced by various nations at certain points in time. Regarding China, Pomeranz held that the contingent factor was the shortage of wood in Britain, something that China did not face, which led Britain to develop mechanization to exploit its deep coal reserves (Pomeranz, 2000). With respect to India, the contingent answer of Parthasarathi was Britain's need to develop the mechanization of textile production to compete with Indian textiles, while Indian exporters did not need such mechanization to be competitive (Parthasarathi, 2011).

Another type of contingency is used to explain Western military superiority. At a general level, the Chinese or Indian empires did not see the need to develop themselves as naval powers; while naval competition among the coastal countries of West Europe led them to develop methods of naval warfare superior to those of the Asian empires (Black, 2015)

We cannot just assume that the material conditions of shortage of wood (or similar reasons) are sufficient to explain the divergence of technology development. This would be the kind of materialism that denies the active element in human history. As Parthasarathi pointed out in his review of Pomeranz, 'The mere existence of resources does not explain the capacity to exploit them' (2002: 284). Technology does not just come into existence because the material conditions require such technology. Knowledge has to be developed.

Parthasarathi has a three-part contingent answer to his question about why Europe and not India grew rich: global competition, deforestation, and state policy (2011: 13). India did not face competition in the global market for cotton textiles. It was Britain that faced the need to break into the market for textiles by developing mechanized processes of production that reduced costs. Britain also faced a shortage of wood for fuel and, developed the coal industry as an alternative, developing systems of deep coal mining using steam power. Finally, unlike the Indian states (Mughal or otherwise), the British state was activist in nature. The state promoted the protection of intellectual property rights, providing monopoly profits to innovators. It also protected British textile manufacturing until mechanization made it cheaper than Indian textiles.

This explanation brings an active element of British trade policy or agency into play in the form of state intervention in economic affairs. The development of knowledge and technology was itself influenced by the needs of British industry with regard to textiles and coal mining. These competitive requirements set the context in which technology developed. However, the technology itself was based on scientific developments, which were chiefly but not exclusively Newtonian mechanics.

The use of steam power to run a set of machines in a factory went beyond the tinkering development of the famous spinning jenny. Spinning jennies could be made without knowledge of mechanical science, but the setting up of factories, in which jennies were connected with steam power, did require knowledge of mechanical science (Jacob, 2014). This mechanical science, whether that of Newton or others, had not been developed as a specific response to such economic requirements. However, it was at hand for use in setting up mechanized factories. The same mechanical science was critical in setting up deep coal mining, which, before steam, was carried out with the organic power of horses, humans, waterwheels, and windmills. These developments were the result of bringing together skilled hands with the knowledge systems (of mechanical science) new to the eighteenth century.

Thus, to promote the supply of science, there must be a demand for science from businesses and the state. Competition in the market economy and the corresponding requirement to be internationally competitive promote the demand for science and its transformation into technology. In capitalism, the push to accumulate is reinforced by the penalty of low share values for non-accumulation. Market competition and the drive to accumulate can also bring about the spread of technological innovations from one sector to another. This is a process that promotes snowballing effects that multiply advantages. Since revolutionizing technology depends on the application of knowledge, there is a sustained demand for the development of knowledge in the competition between firms and countries to get ahead and stay ahead.

At present, it is monopolistic competition and big power rivalry that drive the development of knowledge for technology, particularly the dual-use technology, which can have both civilian and military uses, such as AI. Along with this, there is also the development of technologies that enhance well-being, such as in health, education, and housing.

Taylor (2016) combines the two types of development (international competitiveness and welfare measures) mentioned earlier to analyse the why of S&T or, as termed in this Element, knowledge development; or, why countries differ with respect to the commitment to R&D expenditures. There are two types of conflict that economies or countries face. One is that of internal conflict, such as in the distribution of income between classes, ethnic groups, races or castes. This, according to Taylor, does not require developments in technology. The second is external conflict, which he terms security concerns. Security concerns can be both economic and military. Both of these, however, require an economy to be at the technological frontier and, thus, require investment in R&D and development of S&T.

The balance between internal conflict and security leads to Taylor's creative insecurity, which drives investment in the development of advanced technologies. An economy more concerned with internal conflicts will not invest as much in R&D as one more concerned with external (economic or military) conflicts. The USA had done this earlier in response to the 1950s *Sputnik* fears of falling behind the Soviet Union (Taylor, 2016).

Korea faced an external economic crisis with the Asian Financial Crisis of 1998–1999. It responded with increased investment in R&D from 2000 – R&D expenditure as a percentage of GDP has gone up from 2.02 per cent in 1999 to 4.8per cent in 2020 (World Bank, 2023). China, too, after the 2008 Financial Crisis and the growing big power competition with the USA, responded with a strategy to develop its own technologies with R&D growing from 1.7 per cent in 2010 to 2.4 per cent in 2020 (World Bank, 2023) . On the other hand, India shows a decline from 0.82 per cent in 2009–2010 to 0.64 per cent in 2020 (World Bank, 2023), very much lagging behind the others in this comparison. With South Africa being mainly concerned with the internal conflicts in building a post-Apartheid democracy and facing no meaningful external conflicts could help explain the very low investment of South Africa in trying to be at the technological frontier at 0.68 per cent in 2003 and 0.6 per cent in 2020 (World Bank, 2023). The key Latin American countries all stagnated in this period. Brazil's R&D was higher than that of the others – 1.05 per cent (2000) and 1.15 per cent (2020); while for Argentina it was 0.42 per cent (1996) and 0.52 per cent (2021) and for Mexico) 0.25 per cent (1996) and 0.3 per cent (2020). Only Uruguay doubled its R&D share from 0.27 per cent (1996) to 0.52 per cent (2021).

The high levels of internal conflict in both China and India lead Taylor to be sceptical of whether one of these countries will lead the next technological revolution. The aforementioned data show that this could be true of India, though China does not seem to be similarly affected.

The balance between internal and external conflicts where the latter alone requires sustained efforts at knowledge and technology creation gives a structure to discussions of agency in knowledge creation. But this contrast itself requires some modification. For one, the heightening of external conflicts could itself be a way of dealing with internal conflicts. Further, there can be technological developments even in dealing with internal conflicts. The Indian development of hyper-scale biometric identification and financial delivery systems can be seen as a technological response to internal conflicts.

Nevertheless, Taylor's concept of creative insecurity can be used with some modifications. The main modification is that external conflicts can be related to the drive of monopoly capital and related big power rivalry to establish geographical areas of domination as a driver of expenditure for development on R&D. If we saw in Section 3 that Britain's drive to establish a large enough market for its manufactures provided an economic basis for empire, current monopolistic competition and big power rivalry are factors driving the contemporary development of advanced technologies.

Institutions and the Growth of Knowledge

The why of knowledge development determines the importance given to it in an economy. The how relates to the institutions and incentives that are in place or set up for knowledge development. Much of the discussion on developing the knowledge economy has focused on the how, including questions of culture and social structure. In taking up the how question, a first step, is to move away from the notion that there was just one Scientific Revolution, the one that underlay the Industrial Revolution. Thomas Kuhn (1962) put forward the analysis that there have been and will be numerous scientific revolutions. As empirical evidence accumulates that contradicts an existing paradigm, there will be a push for a new paradigm that better explains both old and new data. Furthermore, the reality that science deals with is itself evolving and even changing reflexively in the Anthropocene. Thus, instead of discovering 'the truth', which is fixed and immutable, science can, at best, make 'less false' statements (Harding, 2013), a process without an end.

As against assumptions of the purely European origins of the Scientific Revolution, many authors point out that Western science borrowed from various types of knowledge in Asia, such as the zero in mathematics from India, gunpowder and printing from China, or navigation from the Ottoman Empire. Jack Goody emphasized this borrowing in *The East in the West* (1996), as did Jack Hobson in *The Eastern Origins of Western Civilization* (2004).

Given this global structure of knowledge production, should we accept a circular or a network approach to analysing the problems of knowledge creation and differential returns to some segments or actors? Kapil Raj argues for a circular approach which, he says, is not, 'a blindly optimistic vision of books, ideas, practices, people and material flowing smoothly between cultures, communities and geographical spaces' (2013: 344). In that case, how do you bring inequality into the uniform curvature of a circle? How do you identify nodes that are able to capture most or much of the profits from knowledge creation?

A network seems to be more appropriate than a circle to characterize the unevenness – both in connectedness and returns – captured from knowledge creation. For instance, taking it for granted that there are numerous actors across geographies in creating quinine or artemisinin in treating malaria, how does one account for the fact that the drug manufacturers capture all of the monopoly profits? These monopoly profits are justified on the basis of their supposed creation of knowledge, which has, in fact, been formed across a number of geographies. There is a two-way flow of knowledge – say, from traditional healers to drug companies and then from drug companies to the consumers of these drugs. However, there is either a minimal flow of knowledge (or none at all) back from the drug companies to the healers, apart from the fact that the drug now replaces the plant. This cannot be called an equal flow. The knowledge that finally results in the drug goes from the traditional healer to the pharmaceutical company or scientist, and the resulting monopoly profits are captured by the pharmaceutical company. This circular analogy does not allow one to capture this inequality, while a network analysis, which can accommodate the 'winner take all' (Giridhardas, 2018) power distribution model, does allow for this inequality.

Strengthening Nodes

The kind of knowledge that passes through a country and can thus be accumulated within it depends very much on the knowledge networks in which it has nodes. Two factors influence the power of networks – size and diversity (Hidalgo, 2015). The size of a network increases with the number of connections and creates feedback loops that amplify knowledge. The diversity of links within a network supports the accumulation of knowledge acquired from different nodes with differing points of view.

This could be applied to the power of nodes within networks. Those nodes that have more and diverse connections have more power than those that have fewer and less diverse connections. Further, modifying Coleman (1988) the size of networks depends on the extent of social connections, both strong and weak. Pre-existing social networks affect the composition of professional networks. These connections can become the base of the new knowledge or epistemic community. At the same time, professional networks as, for instance, that of Silicon Valley, USA, can also lead to a global development of new nodes, as with Bengaluru or Taiwan.

The size of these nodes also depends on the cost of setting them up. Trust reduces the cost of setting up and monitoring networks within nodes. Trust is the expectation that members will do the right thing, irrespective of incentives to do otherwise (Granovetter, 1985). That itself depends on the extent of trust within society as a whole. In low-trust societies, networks tend to be family-based, while in high-trust societies, they can be much broader (Hidalgo, 2015). In addition, weaker social distinctions tend to allow the interaction and integration of disparate components of knowledge, which, according to Renn (2020: 215), was characteristic of science and technology in Western Europe in the early modern period.

Feedback loops, based on the communication between analysts or theorists and artisans or workers, were important in the development of science in Europe: 'whether practical men could have access to propositional knowledge that could serve as the epistemic base for new techniques. It is the strong complementarity, the continued feedback between the two systems of knowledge that set the new course' (Mokyr, 2002: 65).

In contemporary India, however, there are different circuits of knowledge that don't necessarily interact. There are various public sector research institutes under the Council of Scientific and Industrial Research (CSIR), but these don't connect with enterprises, and thus, the needs of businesses could be ignored in setting their research agendas. They are also separate from the teaching departments in the universities. This should be contrasted with the situation in China, where public research institutes were handed over to large business enterprises, as was the case with electronics research and the telecom giant, Huawei (Fan, 2018).

Literacy is important in fostering interaction and developing nodes. The doctrine of the European Reformation held that individuals could, on their own, be in communion with God. This required literacy as individuals should be able to read the Bible in at least one language. The adoption and spread of the Chinese invention of printing in Europe is a testament to the fact that copying books had gone beyond what could be done by hand. It is estimated that some eighty million copies of the Bible were printed in early modern Europe in the period from 1450 to 1600.

On the other hand, though printing was known to the Mughal Empire (and the Ottoman Empire as well), it did not lead to the adoption of printing. This failure to adopt printing in India has been attributed to a desire to protect the profession of scribes, or to 'cultural resistance' (Richards, 1996). Furthermore, until the establishment of British colonial rule, the systematic knowledge of Hindu science, in the Shastras, was confined to the Sanskrit language. This monopoly of men of the Sanskrit-language castes was protected by the existing norms of science, since 'communication outside of Sanskrit was viewed as transgressive' (Pollock, 2011: 351). Persian was used in some contexts, particularly in literature, but the vernaculars were not so used. In contrast, there was a vernacularization of science in Europe where Descartes, Bacon, and Galileo all wrote in their respective vernaculars (Pollock, 2011: 7).

Even in contemporary India, unlike China (or Korea and Japan for that matter) scientific education and scientific discussion are carried out largely in English and not in the vernaculars. This would restrict the communication between artisans and scientists and the transmission of scientific knowledge to the people at large. It is only recently that steps have been taken in promoting science education in the vernaculars.

If language acts as a form of exclusion that restricts interaction, there are also other social relations that act to exclude. Caste, race, and gender are all forms of exclusion. These exclusions were legal at one time – for instance, in ancient India through the caste system and for long afterwards, in the USA till the emancipation of slaves, and in Europe of women from scientific endeavours. While these exclusions were legal at one time, their social strength as norms has continued for long after, right into the contemporary era. These exclusions are important because they restrict both the size of the knowledge community and its diversity. They also restrict the interactions between different knowledge actors. All together, such exclusions restrict the strength of a node.

A companion paper (Nathan, Kelkar and Govindnathan, 2022) looked at the exclusion of women from the core knowledge of most Hindu castes, such as ploughing, turning the potter's wheel, or reciting the Vedic scriptures. Women were also excluded from the development of propositional knowledge from their empirically derived prescriptive knowledge. Women, clearly, would have been the ideal repositories of much prescriptive knowledge of medical treatment, being the primary caregivers at the household level. However, women were excluded from medical education (Chattopadhyaya, 1977) and did not have any role to play in the formulation of the propositional knowledge of Ayurveda – though in South India, the Tamil sage Avvai, who had forsaken female sexuality, is said to have composed a *materia medica*, apart from a book on metaphysics (Chakravarty, 1989: 20).

Overall separation of the various circuits of practical and propositional knowledge restricts the development of knowledge. However, such exclusion of women was not exclusive to India. It existed in Europe as well. Though women practiced medicine, they were not recognized as doctors in early modern France, where the Faculty of Medicine in Paris declared that 'what women did in the process of assisting each other in birth was not considered medicine' (Green, 2008: 323). Overall, science as it developed in Europe was a 'world without women' (Noble, 1992). Such exclusion, whether on the basis of gender, caste, or race, weakens the strength of nodes in knowledge creation. Exclusion both reduces the numbers in networks and truncates the necessary interaction between different circuits of knowledge.

Clusters as Nodes

Within networks, some nodes may develop as clusters as the creation and circulation of knowledge are subject to externalities, resulting in increasing returns where the units are in connection with each other, as in a cluster. This feature of increasing returns, where units are in communication with each other, was first noted by Alfred Marshall, who developed his theory of clusters based on increasing returns where a strong knowledge base is present. Where there is much tacit knowledge, the phenomenon of increasing returns is likely to be even more important (Feldman and Choi, 2015).[3]

It has generally been assumed that clustering is successful where units are of the same type or sector, as in Marshall's analysis. However, in *The Economy of Cities* (1969), Jane Jacobs argued that complementary knowledge from diverse firms promoted the creation of knowledge. This means that diversity, rather than uniformity, would be more conducive to the creation of knowledge. Maryann Feldman and Jongmin Choi (2015) mention studies that show that diversity leads to more creativity than uniformity. Video communication certainly supports communication among diverse sets of persons. However, the formation of such groups from diverse disciplines requires situations where these groups could be formed, such as in college cafeterias or weekend hangout locations. Even within units, much store is now being placed on the role of diversity in fostering creativity.

Authority in Knowledge

Developing knowledge or science requires challenging accepted theories or doctrines. Such a challenge depends on inductive logic and the formulation of generalizations from experiment or observation. In Europe, Francis Bacon was an unmitigated supporter of developing theory from induction, through experiment or observation, and not deductive reasoning (Klein, 2020). This gave impetus to challenging the old theories received from the Greeks and formulating new theories in their place. As we have come to learn from Kuhn's analysis of scientific revolutions, there can be an accumulation of results, observational or experimental, that run counter to the received theory. At some point in time, the weight of counter-examples overwhelms the old theory or paradigm. However, the old theory needs to be replaced by a new theory, which

---

[3] This section owes much to Feldman and Choi (2015).

incorporates the counter-results and does not just leave them as unexplained exceptions. Therefore, those formulating and expounding the new theory have to be ready to challenge the old one. This was witnessed in Europe in the struggle over the Copernican theory, which challenged Aristotle's physics. Later, the theory of the circulation of blood developed by Harvey challenged the Greek medical system of Galen (Goldstone, 2006: 9). What is important is that experiments were used to overturn old theories and formulate new ones.

Jack Goldstone points out that this did not happen in the Chinese, Ottoman, or Indian empires. Though the role of experiment was acknowledged in the Ottoman Empire, 'following extensive internal rebellions, Ottoman religious leaders determined that internal discord was a result of turning away from pure Islam; they, too, turned themselves against innovation as leading only to error, and froze intellectual advance' (Goldstone, 2006: 9).

Similarly, from 1644 onwards, the Manchus of China: 'in order to demonstrate their right to rule, decided to propagate a "pure" form of Confucianism orthodoxy ... all opinions outside of Confucian orthodoxy were banned. Although there was progress in practical areas of agriculture and managing irrigation and flood works, scientific progress and innovation were virtually halted' (Goldstone, 2006: 9).

In India, Debiprasad Chattopadhyaya (1977) argued that unlike in the pre–Common Era period, which saw the foundational writings of Carvaka and Sushruta on medicine, religious orthodoxy during the Gupta Empire in the early centuries of the first millennium inhibited the changing of theories of medicine, despite an accumulation of evidence that went against the foundational theories of Ayurveda. As a Dutch scholar of Indian medicine put it,

> it must be added that it is also one of the basic characteristics of ayurveda that despite this acumen [in observation] and the recognition of numerous exceptions to the theoretical rules, the anomalies observed did not become an incentive for the improvement of the theory or the formulation of supplementary rules. The reason for this stagnation of creative thought may have been the increasing domination of orthodox religion and the power of its representatives. (Meulenbeld, 1987: 4)

Stagnation, then, was not inherent in Indian or other Asian knowledge systems. Rather, it was a result of the politically imposed requirement to conform to religious or state doctrines.

Any empirical formulation is subject to being challenged and negated, according to Karl Popper's analysis (1959). Consequently, it needs to be accepted that knowledge systems sometimes need to be changed and cannot remain immutable. If, however, knowledge has to conform to certain religious or political tenets, then it would not be amenable to changes that challenge some of these tenets or foundational beliefs. The methods of validating knowledge need to be freed from religious or state control. There is a need for restrictions on developing technology, such as current international agreements to restrict development of chemical weapons. AI technology will also require similar restrictions, for instance, on the development of autonomous weapon systems. But similar restrictions on the development of knowledge to conform to religious, bureaucratic, or autocratic tenets would seriously restrict the development and strength of a node within the global network of science.

Cosmopolitanism and Learning

In a network knowledge flows in multiple directions between various nodes. A node gains in importance as it is able to absorb and develop knowledge it receives from other nodes. For instance, the primary knowledge (that the bark of the cinchona tree is a cure for malaria, for example) may be acquired, sometimes even stolen. However, it still has to be developed in terms of isolating the active compound and synthesizing it and manufacturing a tablet. We have referred to Britain's 'long Indian apprenticeship' in learning the implicit knowledge of cotton textile manufacture.

Such apprenticeship or learning, however, requires a cosmopolitan attitude to acquiring knowledge or information from other nodes. Such learning would not be possible with a dismissal of that which is different or novel. In the early modern history of both China and India we find instances of such dismissal of the novel. There is a much-repeated story of the Chinese emperor in 1793 writing that China had everything and did not need such things from others (Harrison, 2017).

Learning is also inhibited by the hubris of thinking that we know or knew it all. At the time of the G-20 summit in Delhi in 2023, there was an advertising blitz touting India as a 'Vishwaguru' or 'teacher to the world' (Aiyar, 2023). Such hubris does not go along with the need to absorb knowledge from all over the world needed to increase the weight and importance of a node in a network.

7 Conclusions

This Element argues that the enclosure or monopolization of advanced technological knowledge works in conjunction with development policies to create inequality between countries in the global capitalist economy. In support of the aforementioned analysis of the present (of global inequality) as history (of unequal access to knowledge) there is the finding of Weber et al. (2022) – that export complexity, or in our terms, knowledge content of production, of a country in 1897–1906 is a good predictor of rank in per capita income in 1998-2007, with a few notable exceptions.

This history is interrogated in two ways. First, as a history of colonial and, later, neoliberal (or market fundamentalist) policy over two centuries. The second interrogation of history is in identifying the movement from the use to the creation of knowledge as the way out of the middle-income trap.

The contemporary global economic structure should not be seen as just a continuation of the colonial structure. There are connections between the two, particularly in creating the ex-colonies as countries of low per capita income and low wages. However, the contemporary global economic structure has its own way of knowledge-based inequality, characteristically through the division of knowledge and labour between headquarter and supplier firms in GVCs, in creating and perpetuating global inequality. This contemporary global capitalist structure is interrogated through a Southern lens in terms of the structural change from use to creation of knowledge needed to overcome global economic inequality.

In the contemporary global structure, we identified three sources of knowledge-based growth for economies of the Global South – economies that are intertwined with the Global North in terms of divisions of knowledge and, thus, labour. The first is that of growth largely within the contours of the existing division of the creation and use of knowledge, concentrating on the use of relatively commoditized production knowledge and growing in scale. The second is the development of managerial and labour capabilities and the development of intermediate technological capabilities, taking on more functions in a movement from straightforward assembly to full-package supply. The third is the movement into products that are based on new knowledge and innovation.

However, the movement from middle-income to high-income status involves the development of headquarters firms based on the third source of growth, the creation of monopolized knowledge or the formation of intellectual monopoly capital. This requires a qualitative change in the knowledge economy, from an emphasis on learning to use and adapt knowledge to the creation of knowledge that can be monopolized and combined with monopsony, as the new headquarter firms build their own global value chains with support from their states.

Thus, with such monopolized knowledge, the creation of headquarter firms that can earn excess profits becomes possible, along with that of suppliers of high-value services. This is the major discontinuity or non-linearity in the process of vertically specialized industrialization. It is this necessity for a strategy and investment in the development of the knowledge economy that introduces a non-linear dynamic into the model of vertically specialized industrialization. While this development of the knowledge economy will have a substantial element of techno-nationalism, its success also becomes the basis for geo-strategic competition for spheres of influence, investment, and markets, pitting emerging headquarters firms against older established firms and economies. Emerging economies will also be pitted against each other, as they try to build their own markets of intellectual monopoly capitalism and zones of monopsony.

The world is clearly in the throes of such an ongoing struggle for the redistribution and defence of spaces of domination, augmenting the crisis of climate change with this conflict. The inter-twining of these two crises is seen in the energy struggles around Russia's war in Ukraine, which has already pushed many countries to increase reliance on coal-fired energy. This makes it even more urgent to search for sustainable alternatives to the capitalist development of the current intellectual monopoly-cum-monopsony variety. Since the basis of intellectual monopoly capitalism is the monopolization of knowledge through the system of intellectual property rights, an alternative can be created by changing the system of intellectual property rights that now produces pervasive monopolies.

Reforming the Knowledge Economy

The usual argument in favour of higher returns for intellectual monopolies is that they provide incentives for knowledge produced by firms. However, by seeing the co-production of the knowledge in these products, we can expose the incorrectness of this single-agent argument, irrespective of whether that refers to scientists or firms. Arrow refers to the social character of knowledge production (1994). Mazzucatto argues that the system of developing technological knowledge is collective, involving both public and private actors (2013). What needs to be recognized is that the social or collective character is and has been global. Neither methodological individualism nor methodological nationalism is an adequate approach to knowledge creation.

In a product, knowledge, made with multiple actors across geographies, one way of apportioning the combined returns is on the basis of the costs of production, with allowance made for risk-taking. Therefore, scientific effort (by individuals or firms) should be rewarded, the way all other production is rewarded – costs plus the normal or competitive profit, with an allowance for risk-taking. Scientific effort, the creation of knowledge, and its translation into business innovation are always risky. For that reason, Marx, Schumpeter and Perez all emphasize the need for rewarding risk-taking. Sen (2004) points to the need to provide an incentive for knowledge creation in a well-functioning society. Currently the incentive of intellectual property rights creates intellectual monopoly capitalism and impedes the beneficial spread of technology.

What is needed is a system of incentives without the creation of intellectual monopoly capital.

Intellectual property rights law needs to be based on an appropriate notion of costs and rewards for risk-taking while allowing for the quickest and widest spread of that knowledge and technology so as to reduce global inequality. A system of incentive without monopoly can be one of compulsory licensing but not monopoly, with fees based on an estimate of R&D costs with a return of, say, 10 per cent, and an addition for risk-taking (Kingston, 2001). In case additional incentives are required, that could be provided through subsidies instead of national and international legally supported intellectual monopolies (Boldrin and Levine, 2008: 258).

Such compulsory licensing will not act like a magic wand in eliminating global inequality – we will still need to develop knowledge and technological capabilities in the Global South to absorb (and not just use) technological knowledge and to develop new technological knowledge from that. However, it can be a way to begin the transformation of intellectual monopoly capitalism and speed up the reduction of global inequality. A good example of this global transformation is that of the development of Indian generic drug production with weak intellectual property rights protection (only process but not product patents) during the pre-WTO period, which substantially brought down the costs of treatment during the HIV-AIDS pandemic. A system of compulsory licensing would promote the global use of knowledge and the attendant build-up of technological capabilities in the Global South.

While making the case for a switch to compulsory licensing, it would be more possible to build a political coalition for trying this out in the case of critical health and climate-friendly technologies. With the global inequalities in the COVID pandemic still with us, and the ongoing climate change crisis showing no signs of relenting, a global political coalition could be built to support such a change in intellectual property rights for critical health and climate-friendly technologies. Of course, there are strong lobbies in favour of the continuation of intellectual property rights, as seen in the opposition to the India–South Africa initiative to set up compulsory licensing for COVID-19 vaccinations. Nevertheless, critical health and climate-friendly technologies are areas for which political coalitions could be built for compulsory licensing, which could then be extended to new areas. A new political economy is required, but we can begin with relatively small steps.

References

Abu-Lughold, Janet. (1989). Before European Hegemony: The World System A.D. 1250–1350. Oxford: Oxford University Press.

Aiyar, Swaminathan. (2023). India Is Not the World's Guru. *Nikkei Asia*. September 8. https://asia.nikkei.com/Opinion/India-s-Modi-is-not-the-world-s-guru, last accessed January 6, 2024. https://ora.ox.ac.uk/objects/uuid:11ae6240-8b0f-45f3-ab5e-4a8dbfb676f6.

Allen, Robert C. (2007). Engels' Pause: A Pessimist's Guide to the British Industrial Revolution, University of Oxford, Department of Economics, Discussion Paper Series, last accessed 13 December 2022.

Amin, Samir. (1974). Accumulation on a World Scale. New York: Monthly Review Press.

Amsden, Alice. (2001). The Rise of the Rest. Oxford: Oxford University Press.

Appadurai, Arjun. (2022). Email to Dev Nathan, 13 July 2022.

Appadurai, Arjun. (1990). Disjuncture and Difference in the Global Cultural Economy. Theory, Culture and Society, 7 (2–3), 295–310.

Arocena, Rodrigo and Judith Sutz. (2010). Weak Knowledge in the South: Innovation Policies and Knowledge Divides. Science and Public Policy, 37 (8), 571–582.

Arrow, K. J. (1962). The Economic Implications of Learning by Doing. The Review of Economic Studies, 29 (3), 155–173.

Arrow, K. J. (1994). Methodological Individualism and Social Knowledge. American Economic Review, 84 (2), 1–9.

Arrow, K. J. (1999). Knowledge as a Factor of Production. World Bank Development Research Conference. Washington, DC: The World Bank.

Bagchi, Amiya. (1976). De-Industrialization of India in the Nineteenth Century: Some Theoretical Implications. Journal of Development Studies, 12 (2), 153–174.

Bauer, P. T. (1953). Concentration in Tropical Trade: Some Aspects and Implications of Oligopoly. Economica, *New Series*, 20 (80), 302–321.

Bhatia, Lakshmi. (2023). Personal communication, July 1.

Black, Jeremy. (2015). Patterns of Warfare. In Jerry Bentley, Sanjay Subrahmanyam and Merry Weisner-Hanks, eds., The Cambridge World History, Vol. VI: The Construction of a Global World, Cambridge: Cambridge University Press, pp. 29–49.

Boldrin, Michele and David Levine. (2008). Against Intellectual Monopoly. Cambridge: Cambridge University Press.

Boyle, James. (2003). The Second Enclosure Movement and the Construction of the Public Domain. Law and Contemporary Problems, 66 (33), 33–74.

Broadberry, Stephen, Rainer Fremdling and Peter Solar. (2010). Industry. In Stephen Broadberry and Kevin H. O'Rourke, eds., The Cambridge Economic History of Modern Europe, *Vol. 1*, Cambridge: Cambridge University Press, pp. 165–187.

Chakraborty, Shouvik and Prabirjit Sarkar. (2020). From the Classical Economists to Empiricists: A Review of the Terms of Trade Controversy. Journal of Economic Reviews, 34 (5), 1111–1133.

Chan, Jenny, Pun Ngai and Mark Selden. (2016). The Politics of Global Production: Apple, Foxconn and China's New Working Class. In Dev Nathan, Meenu Tewari and Sandip Sarkar, eds., Labour in Global Value Chains in Asia, Cambridge: Cambridge University Press, pp. 353–376.

Chang, Ha-Joon. (2000). Kicking Away the Ladder: Development Policy in Historical Perspective. London: Anthem Press.

Chang, Ha-Joon and Kiryl Zach. (2019). Industrialization and Development. In Deepak Nayyar, ed., Asian Transformations: An Enquiry into the Development of Nations, Oxford: Oxford University Press, pp. 186–215.

Chakravarty, Uma. (1989). The World of the Bhaktin in South Indian Traditions – The Body and Beyond. Manushi, 50 (52), 18–28.

Chattopadhyaya, Debiprasad. (1977). Science and Civilization in Ancient India. Calcutta: K. P. Bagchi.

Cohen, Wesley and Daniel Levinthal. (1989). Innovation and Learning: The Two Phases of R&D. Economic Journal, 99, 569–596

Coleman, James. (1988). Social Capital in the Creation of Human Capital. American Journal of Sociology, 94, S95–120.

D'Cruz, Premila. (2012). Workplace Bullying in India. London: Routledge.

De Marchi, Valentina, Eleonora Di Maria and Gary Gereffi. (2018). Local Clusters in Global Value Chains. London: Routledge.

Degain, Christophe, Bo Meng and Zhi Wang. (2017). Recent Trends in Global Trade and Global Value Chains. In Global Value Chain Development Report 2017: Measuring and Analyzing the Impact of GVCs on Economic Development, Washington, DC: The World Bank, pp. 37–68.

Drezner, Daniel, Henry Farrell and Abraham Newman, eds. (2021). The Uses and Abuses of Weaponized Interdependence. Washington, DC: Brookings Institution.

Durand, Cedric and William Milberg. (2019). Intellectual Monopoly in Global Value Chains. Review of International Political Economy, 27 (2), 404–429. https://doi.org/10.1080/09692290.2019.1660703.

Dutt, R. C. [1901 (1994)]. The Economic History of India. Delhi: Low Price Publications.

Ernst, Dieter. (2012). Europe's Innovation Union – Beyond Techno-Nationalism? *East-West Center Working Paper, Economics Series*, No. 132. Accessed 10 October, 2023, http://128.171.57.22/bitstream/10125/24414/econwp132.pdf.

Fan, Pei Lei. (2018). Innovation and Learning of Latecomers: A Case Study of Chinese Telecom Equipment Companies. In Dev Nathan, Meenu Tewari and Sandip Sarkar, eds., Development with GVCs: Innovation and Upgrading in Asia, Cambridge: Cambridge University Press, pp. 157–175.

Feldman, Maryann and Jongmin Choi. (2015). Harnessing the Geography of Innovation: Toward Evidence-Based Economic Development Policy. In Daniele Archibhgi and Andrea Fillipetti, eds., The Handbook of Global Science, Technology and Innovation, London: John Wiley and Sons, pp. 269–289.

Feldman, Robin. (2018). May Your Drug Price Be Evergreen. Journal of Law and the Biosciences, 5 (3), 590–647.

Findlay, Robert. (2019). Asia and the World Economy in Historical Perspective. In Deepak Nayyar, ed., Asian Transformations: An Enquiry into the Development of Nations, Oxford: Oxford University Press, pp. 80–108.

Freeman, Christopher. (2007). The Political Economy of the Long Wave. In Geoffrey Hodson, ed., The Evolution of Economic Institutions, London: Edward Elgar, pp. 75–97.

Gill, Indermit and Homi Kharas. (2007). An East Asian Renaissance: Ideas for Economic Growth. Washington, DC: The World Bank.

Giridhardas, Anand. (2018). Winners Take All: The Elite Charade of Changing the World. New York: Alfred A. Knopf.

Goldstone, Jack. (2006). Knowledge – Not Capitalism, Faith, or Reason – Was the Key to 'The Rise of the West'. Historically Speaking, 7 (4), 6–10.

Goodall, Jane. (1971). In the Shadow of Man. New York: Houghton, Mifflin and Harcourt.

Goody, Jack. (1996). The East in the West. Cambridge: Cambridge University Press.

Grabs, Janina and Stefano Ponte. (2019). The Evolution of Power in the Global Coffee Value Chain and Production Network. Journal of Economic Geography, 19, 803–828.

Granovetter, Mark. (1985). Economic Action and Social Structure: The Problem of Embeddedness. American Journal of Sociology, 91 (3), 481–910.

Green, Maya. (2008). Making Women's Medicine Masculine: The Rise of Male Authority in Premodern Gynaecology. Oxford: Oxford University Press.

Grilli, E. R. and M. C. Yang. (1988). Primary Commodities Prices, Manufactured Goods Prices and the Terms of Trade of Developing Countries: What the Long Run Shows. World Bank Economic Review, 2 (1), 1–47.

Grinin, Leonid and Andrey Korotayev. (2015). Great Divergence and Great Convergence: A Global Perspective. Geneva: Springer International.

Harding, Sandra. (2013). The Less False Accounts of Feminist Standpoint Epistemology. In Jason Hannan, ed., Philosophical Profiles in the Theory of Communication, New York: Peter Lang.

Harrison, Henrietta. (2017). The Qianlong Emperor's Letter to George III and the Early Twentieth-Century Origins of Ideas about China's External Relations. The American Historical Review, 122 (3), 680–201.

Hidalgo, Cesar. (2015). Why Information Grows. New York: Hachette Books.

Hidalgo, Cesar and Ricardo Hausmann. (2009). The Building Blocks of Economic Complexity. Proceedings of the National Academy of Sciences, 106 (26), 10570–10576.

Hippe, Ralph and Roger Fouquet. (2018). The Knowledge Economy in Historical Perspective. World Economics, 18 (1), 75–107.

Hobson, John. (2004). The Eastern Origins of Western Civilization. Cambridge: Cambridge University Press.

Im, Fernando Gabriel and David Rosenblatt. (2013). Middle-Income Traps: A Conceptual and Empirical Survey. Policy Research Working Paper 6594. The World Bank.

Jacob, Jane. (1969). The Economy of Cities. New York: Random House.

Jacob, Margaret. (2014). The First Knowledge Economy. Cambridge: Cambridge University Press.

Jannace, William and Paul Tiffany. (2019). A New World Order: The Rule of Law, or the Law of Rulers? Fordham International Law Journal, 42 (5), 1979–2019.

Jeremy, David J. (1977). Damming the Flood: British Government Efforts to Check the Outflow of Technicians and Machinery, 1780–1843. The Business History Review, 51 (1), 1–34.

Kalecki, Michal. (1971). Class Struggle and the Distribution of National Income. Kyklos, 24 (1), 1–9.

Kaplinsky, Raphael and Mike Morris. (2001). A Handbook of Value Chain Research. University of Cape Town, www.researchgate.net/publication/42791981_A_Handbook_for_Value_Chain_Research, last accessed 3 July 2022.

Kaplinsky, Raphael. (2019). Rents and Inequality in Global Value Chains. In Stefano Ponte, Gary Gereffi and Gale Raj-Reichert, eds., Handbook of Global Value Chains, London: Edward Elgar, pp. 153–168.

Kathuria, Vinish. (2002). Liberalisation, FDI and Productivity Spillovers – An Analysis of Indian Manufacturing Firms. Oxford Economic Paper, 54, 688–718.

Kelkar, Govind, Girija Shrestha and Veena N. (2002). IT Industry and Women's Agency. Gender, Technology and Development, 6 (1), 62–84.

Kelly, Lynne. (2015). Knowledge and Power in Pre-Historic Societies. Cambridge: Cambridge University Press.

Kepe, Marta, Elina Treyger, Christian Curriden et al. (2023). Great Power Conflict and Competition in Africa. Santa Monica, CA: The Rand Corporation. https://doi.org/10.7249/RRA969-2.

Kingston, William. (2001). Meeting Nelson's Concerns about Intellectual Property. https://citeseerx.ist.psu.edu/document?repid=rep1&type=pdf& doi=6930456d4963975b43a4f962d6551e4dad4bde86, last accessed 24 July, 2023.

Klein, Jürgen. (2020). Francis Bacon. The Stanford Encyclopedia of Philosophy (Fall 2020 Edition), Edward N. Zalta (ed.), Stanford University. https://plato .stanford.edu/archives/fall2020/entries/francis-bacon/.

Krugman, Paul, (1979). A Model of Innovation, Technology Transfer, and the World Distribution of Income. Journal of Political Economy, 87 (2), 253–266.

Kuhn, Thomas. [1962 (2012)]. The Structure of Scientific Revolutions. Chicago: University of Chicago Press.

Kumar, Ashok. (2020). Monopsony Capitalism: Power and Production in the Twilight of the Sweatshop Age. Cambridge: Cambridge University Press.

Kuznets, Simon. (1965). Economic Growth and Structure. New York: Norton

Lall, Sanjaya. (1992). Technological Capabilities and Industrialization. World Development, 20 (2), 165–186.

Lall, Sanjaya. (2000). The Technological Structure and Performance of Developing Country Manufactured Exports, 1985-1998. Oxford Development Studies, 28 (3), 317–369.

Lee, Kuen. (2013). Schumpeterian Analysis of Economic Catch-Up: Knowledge, Path Creation and the Middle-Income Trap. Cambridge: Cambridge University Press.

Lenin, V. I. [1917 (1966)]. Imperialism, the Highest Stage of Capitalism. Moscow: Foreign Languages Publishing House.

Luxemburg, Rosa. (1951). The Accumulation of Capital. New York: Monthly Review Press.

Lewis, W. Arthur. (1978). The Evolution of the International Economic Order. Princeton: Princeton University Press.

Maddison, Angus. (2007). The World Economy. OECD, Delhi: Academic Foundation.

Mani, Sunil. (2023). Innovation Performance of India's Computer Ssoftware Services and Pharmaceutical Manufacturing Industries. Economic and Political Weekly, 58 (47), 45–54.

Marx, Karl. (1848). *Manifesto of the Communist Party.* www.marxists.org/archive/marx/works/1848/communist-manifesto/ch01.htm.

Marx, Karl. (1852). *The Eighteenth Brumaire of Louis Bonaparte.* www.marxists.org/archive/marx/works/1852/18th-brumaire/ch01.htm

Mazzucato, Mariana. (2013). The Entrepreneurial State. London: Anthem Press.

Milanovic, Branko. (2018). Global Inequality. Cambridge, MA: Harvard University Press.

Milanovic, Branko. (2023). The Great Convergence: Global Equality and Its Discontents. *Foreign Affairs*, July–August. www.foreignaffairs.com/world/great-convergence-equality-branko-milanovic.

Miller, Chris. (2022). Chip War: The Fight for the World's Most Critical Technology. New York: Scribner.

Morishima, Michio. (1982). Why Has Japan Succeeded? Cambridge: Cambridge University Press.

Mei, Lixia and Jici Wang. (2016). Dynamics of Labour-Intensive Clusters in China: Wage Costs and Moving Inland. In Dev Nathan, Meenu Tewari and Sandip Sarkar, eds., Labour in Global Value Chains in Asia, Cambridge: Cambridge University Press. pp. 183–211.

Meulenbeld, G. Jan. (1987). Reflections on the Basic Concept of Indian Pharmacology. In G. Van Meulenbeld and Dominik Wujastyk, eds., Studies on Indian Medical History, Delhi: Motilal Banarsidas, pp. 1–16.

Milberg, Will and Deborah Winkler. (2013). Outsourcing Economics. Cambridge: Cambridge University Press.

Mokyr, Joel. (2002). The Gifts of Athena. Oxford: Oxford University Press.

Mokyr, Joel and Hans-Joachim Voth. (2010). Understanding Growth in Europe, 1700-1870.: Theory and Evidence. In Stephen Broadberry and Kevin H. O'Rourke, eds., The Cambridge Economic History of Modern Europe, *Vol. 1*, Cambridge: Cambridge University Presss, pp. 7–42.

Naoroji, Dadabhai. [1902 (1988)]. Poverty and Un-British Rule in India. New Delhi: Publications Division, Government of India.

Nathan, Dev. (2016). Governance Types and Employment Systems. In Dev Nathan, Meenu Tewari and Sandip Sarkar, eds., Labour in Global Value Chains in Asia, Cambridge: Cambridge University Press, pp. 479–501.

Nathan, Dev. (2018). GVCs and Development Policy: Vertically Specialized Industrialization. In Dev Nathan, Meenu Tewari and Sandip Sarkar, eds., Development with Global Value Chains: Innovation and Upgrading in Asia, Cambridge: Cambridge University Press, pp. 373–408.

Nathan, Dev. (2020). Knowledge, Oligopoly and Labour in GVCs. Global Labour Journal, 11 (2),134–151.

Nathan, Dev. (2021). From Monopoly to Monopsony Capitalism. Indian Journal of Labour Economics, 64, 843–866.

Nathan, Dev. (2023). Knowledge and Global Inequality: Monopoly-cum-Monopsony Capitalism. Economic and Political Weekly, Feb. 18, 58 (7), 36–44.

Nathan, Dev, Madhuri Saripalle and L. Gurunathan. (2016). Labour Practices in India. ILO Asia-Pacific Working Paper Series.

Nathan, Dev, Meenu Tewari and Sandip Sarkar, eds. (2016). Labour in Global Value Chains in Asia. Cambridge: Cambridge University Press.

Nathan, Dev, Shikha Silliman Bhattacharjee, S. Rahul et al. (2022). Reverse Subsidies in Global Monopsony Capitalism. Cambridge: Cambridge University Press.

Nathan, Dev, Govind Kelkar and Pallavi Govindnathan. (2022). Knowledge and Gender Inequality. Gender, Technology and Development, October, 26 (3), 341–356.

Nathan, Dev, S. Rahul, Joonkoo Lee et al. (2024). Knowledge and Education in Upgrading. (forthcoming).

Nayyar, Deepak. (2019). Resurgent Asia: Diversity in Development. Oxford: Oxford University Press.

Needham, Joseph. (1969). The Grand Titration: Science and Society in East and West. Toronto: University of Toronto Press.

Niti Aayog. (2020). National Strategy for Artificial Intelligence. New Delhi: Niti Aayog.

Noble, David. (1992). A World Without Women: Christian Clerical Science in Western Europe. New York: Knopf.

North, Douglass and Robert Paul West. (1973). The Rise of the Western World: A New Economic History. Cambridge: Cambridge University Press.

O'Rourke, Kevin, Leandro Prados de la Escosura and Guillaume Daudin. (2010). Trade and Empire. In Stephen Broadberry and Kevin H. O'Rourke, eds., The Cambridge Economic History of Modern Europe, *Vol. 1*, Cambridge: Cambridge University Press, pp. 96–121.

OECD. (2013). Supporting Investment in Knowledge Capital, Growth and Innovation. Paris: OECD.

OECD. (2017). Skills and GVCs. www.oecd-ilibrary.org/sites/9789264273351-5-en/index.html?itemId=/content/component/9789264273351-5-en.

OECD. (2020). The Trade Policy Implications of Global Value Chains. www.oecd.org/trade/topics/global-value-chains-and-trade/, last accessed 12 September 2023.

Ostrom, E., P. Gardner and J. Walker. (1994). Rules, Games and Common Pool Resources. Ann Arbor: The University of Michigan Press.

Ostry, Sylvia and Richard Nelson. (1995). Techno-Nationalism and Techno-Globalism: Conflict and Cooperation. Washington, DC: The Brookings Institution.

Oughton, Christine and Damian Tobin. (2023). Joan Robinson: Early Endogenous Growth Theorist. Cambridge Journal of Economics, 47, 943–964.

Pagano, Ugo. (2015). The Crisis of Intellectual Monopoly Capitalism. Cambridge Journal of Economics, 38, 1409–1429.

Palmedo, Michael. (2021). Evaluating the impact of data exclusivity on the price per kilogram of pharmaceutical products. Global Development Policy Center: Boston University. www.bu.edu/gdp/files/2021/04/GEGI_WP_048_Palmedo_FIN.pdf.

Pamuk, Sevket and Jab-Luiten van Zelden. (2010). Standard of Living. In Stephen Broadberry and Kevin H. O'Rourke, eds., The Cambridge Economic History of Modern Europe, *Vol. 1*, Cambridge: Cambridge University Press, pp. 220–235.

Parthasarathi, Prasannan. (2002). Review, the Great Divergence. Past and Present, 176, 275–293.

Parthasarathi, Prasannan. (2011). Why Europe Grew Rich and Asia Did Not: Global Economic Divergence, 1600–1850. Cambridge: Cambridge University Press.

Pattnaik, P. (1997). Accumulation and Stability under Capitalism. Oxford: Clarendon Press.

Paus, Eva and Michael Robinson. (2022). Frim-Level Innovation, Government Policies and the Middle-Income Trap: Insights from Five Latin American Countries. CEPAL Review, 137, 97–120.

Perez, Carlota. (2002). Technological Revolutions and Finance Capital. London: Edward Elgar.

Phillips, Nicola. (2017). Power and Inequality in the Global Economy. International Affairs, 93 (2), 429–444.

Pietrobelli, Carlo and Roberta Rabellotti. (2011). Global Value Chains Meet Innovation Systems: Are There Learning Opportunities for Developing Countries? World Development, 39 (7), 1261–1269.

Piketty, Thomas. (2013). Capital in the Twenty-first Century. Cambridge, MA: Harvard University Press.

Polanyi, Michael. (1966). The Tacit Dimension. Chicago: University of Chicago Press.

Pollock, Stephen. (2011). The Languages of Science in Early Modern India. Forms of Knowledge in Early Modern Asia. Durham, NC: Duke University, 19–48.

Pomeranz, Kenneth. (2000). The Great Divergence: China, Europe and the Making of the World Economy. Princeton: Princeton University Press.

Popper, Karl. (1959). The Logic of Scientific Discovery. London: Routledge.

Prebisch, Raul. (1950). The Economic Development of Latin America and Its Principal Problems. New York: United Nations.

PWC. (2022). Global Top 100 Companies by Market Capitalization. www.pwc .com/gx/en/audit-services/publications/top100/pwc-global-top-100-compan ies-by-market-capitalisation-2022.pdf, last accessed 28 June 2022.

Raj, Kapil. (2007). Circulation and the Construction of Knowledge in South Asia and Europe, 1650 to 1900. London: Palgrave Macmillan.

Raj, Kapil. (2013). Beyond Postcolonialism . . . and Postpositivism: Circulation and the Global History of Science. Isis, 104 (2), 337–347.

Raj-Reichert, Gale. (2018). The Changing Landscape of Contract Manufacturers in the Electronics Industry in Asia. In Dev Nathan, Meenu Tewari and Sandip Sarkar, eds., Development with Global Value Chains: Upgrading and Innovation in Asia, Cambridge: Cambridge University Press, pp. 20–62.

Rand Corporation. (2023). *Great Power Competition and Conflict in Africa.* Santa Monica, CA: Rand Corporation. www.rand.org/content/dam/rand/ pubs/research_reports/RRA900/RRA969-2/RAND_RRA969-2.pdf.

Renn, Juergen. (2020). The Evolution of Knowledge. Princeton: Princeton University Press.

Richards, John. (1996). Early Modern India and World History. Journal of World History, 8 (2), 197–209.

Riello, Giorgio. (2009). The Indian Apprenticeship: The Trade of Indian Textiles and the Making of European Cotton. In Georgio Rielo and Tirthankar Roy, ed., How India Clothed the World, London: Brill, pp. 309–340.

Rikap, Cecilia and Bengt-Ake Lundvall. (2021). The Digital Innovation Race: Conceptualizing the Emerging New Economic Order. London: Palgrave Macmillan.

Robinson, Joan. [1933 (1987)]. The Economics of Imperfect Competition. London: Macmillan.

Romer, Paul. (1990). Endogenous Technical Change. Journal of Political Economy, 98, S71–S102.

Roy, Tirthankar. (2020). The Economic History of India, 1857-2010. Delhi: Oxford University Press.

Sarkar, Sandip and Balwant Mehta. (2016). What Do Workers Get from Being in a GVC? ICT in India. In Dev Nathan, Meenu Tewari and Sandip Sarkar, eds., Labour in Global Value Chains in Asia, Cambridge: Cambridge University Press. pp. 450–478.

Schumpeter, Joseph. [1944 (1976)]. Capitalism, Socialism and Democracy. London: Allen and Unwin.

Sen, Amartya. (2004). Merit and Justice. In Arrow, Kenneth, Samuel Bowles and Stephen Durlauf, eds., Meritocracy and Inequality, Princeton: Princeton University Press. pp. 5–16.

Siddharthan, N. S. (2021). Technology, Globalisation and Multinationals: The Asian Experience. eSocialSciences. http://esocialsciences.org/eBook/eBook_Siddharthan.pdf.

Solow, Robert. (1957). Technical Change and the Aggregate Production Function. Review of Economics and Statistics, 39, 312–320.

Suleyman, Mustafa. (2023). The Coming Wave. London: The Bodley Head.

Syverson, Chad. (2019). Macroeconomics and Market Power: Context, Implications and Open Questions. Journal of Economic Perspectives, 33 (3), 23–43.

Taylor, Mark. (2016). The Politics of Innovation. Oxford: Oxford University Press.

Teece, David. (1986). Profiting from Technological Innovation. Research Policy, 15 (6), 285–305.

Teece, David, Gary Pisano and Amy Schuen. (1997). Dynamic Capabilities and Strategic Management. Strategic Management Journal, 18 (7), 500–533.

Therborn, Goran. (2013). The Killing Fields of Inequality. Cambridge: Polity.

Tokatli, Nebahat. (2014). 'Made in Italy? Who Cares!' Prada's New Economic Geography. Geoforum, 54, 1–9.

Toye, John and Richard Toye. (2008). The Origins and Interpretation of the Prebisch-Singer Thesis. *History of Political Economy*, ORE, Open Research Exeter. http://handle.net/10036/25832, last accessed 20 November 2022.

Tyabji, Nasir. (1995). The Genesis of Chemical-based Industrialization: Oilseeds in Madras. In Roy MacLeod and Deepak Kumar, eds., Technology and the Raj, Delhi: Aakar Books, pp. 78–111.

Tyabji, Nasir. (2018). From the Phased Manufacturing Programme to Frugal Engineering: Some Initial Propositions. In Dev Nathan, Meenu Tewari, and Sandip Sarkar, eds., Development with Global Value Chains: Innovation and Upgrading in Asia. Cambridge: Cambridge University Press, pp. 176–192.

Vaidhyanathan, Siva. (2017). Intellectual Property: A Very Short Introduction. Oxford: Oxford University Press.

Vernon, Raymond. (1966). International Investment and International Trade in the Product Cycle. Quarterly Economic Review, 80 (May), 190–207.

Wallerstein, Immanuel. (2004). World Systems Analysis: An Introduction. Durham, NC: Duke University Press.

Weber, Isabelle, Gregor Semienluk, Junshang Laing and Tom Westland. (2022). Persistence in world export patterns and productive capabilities across two globalizations. Working Paper No. 2022–11, University of Massachusetts, Department of Economics, Amherst, MA.

Williams, Eric. [1944 (1964)]. Capitalism and Slavery. London: A. Deutsch

World Bank. (2015). Poland's Integration and Economic Upgrading in Global Value Chains. Washington, DC: World Bank Group.

World Bank. (2020). World Development Indicators: Science and Technology. Washington, DC: World Bank Group.

World Bank. (2023). Country Income Classifications. https://blogs.worldbank .org/opendata/new-world-bank-country-classifications-income-level-2022-2023, last accessed 15 September 2023.

World Intellectual Property Organization (WIPO). (2021). Global Innovation Index *2021*. Geneva: WIPO. www.wipo.int/edocs/pubdocs/en/wipo_pub_gii_2021.pdf, last accessed 18 June 2022.

Yuan, Xiaodong and Xiaotao Li. (2021). Mapping the Technology Diffusion of Battery Electric Vehicle Based on Patent Analysis. Energy, 222, 1–13

Acknowledgements

The Southern Center for Inequality Studies (SCIS) at WITS University, Johannesburg, supported the completion of this monograph with a Cameron Schrier Equality Fellowship. My thanks to Imraan Valodia for his personal and institutional support.

Thanks to Kunal Sen and the Board of Editors of UNU-WIDER for accepting this monograph to be included in the Cambridge University Press Elements series on Development Economics. A Visiting Scholar position at The New School for Social Research, New York, gave me access to its vast electronic library resources and a chance to have regular discussions with Will Milberg.

Several parts that have gone into making this monograph have been published by *Economic and Political Weekly*, the Institute for Human Development and the Heilbroner Center for the Study of Capitalism at The New School for Social Research. I have drawn on work I did as part of the Capturing the Gains research project and subsequently with the Cambridge University Press GVC series. I have also drawn on work with the International Labour Organization (ILO) and the Asian Development Bank (ADB) for which thanks to Sher Verick and Rana Hasan respectively. The editors and a reviewer of the *Global Labor Journal* nudged me to move from the complexity or otherwise of knowledge to the economic characteristics of knowledge, leading to the distinction between knowledge that is monopolized or in the commons.

Lectures and presentations at TISS, JNU, IIT Bombay, IIM Ahmedabad, Flame University, Bucknell University, Centurion Technical University, at the 2022 Knowledge Conference and several conferences organized by the Institute for Human Development (IHD) and the Institute for Studies in Industrial Development (ISID) and the attendant comments have all helped to formulate and refine my analysis. A pre-publication webinar organized by SCIS and IHD also helped refine the analysis. Thanks to Eddie Webster, Rakesh Besant, K.P. Kannan, Jeemol Unni, and other participants for their comments. Two anonymous reviewers also pointed to areas where the arguments needed to be strengthened or even re-formulated. They also provided apt summaries that I have used. Over time, I have benefitted from discussions with Gerry Rodgers, Dipankar Gupta and Alakh Sharma on various related topics.

Right in the beginning of my endeavour, Sandra Harding encouraged me to pursue this connection between knowledge and inequality. I have relied very heavily on comments from Raphie Kaplinsky, Arjun Appadurai, and Will Milberg. John Pickles, Indira Munshi, Smita Mishra-Panda, Akeel Bilgrami,

Rehman Sobhan, and Nitin Desai commented on various notes leading to this Element. Arjun gave me detailed comments on the difficult section on the knowledge economy, though, of course, he may well disagree with parts of that analysis. Rahul, Joonkoo Lee, Shengjun Zhu and Lauren Johnston have all worked with me in carrying forward some of this analysis. I thank them for permission to use some of the cross-country data they have painstakingly put together. While all of the aforementioned have contributed to my analysis, none of them bears any responsibility for any errors and the analysis itself. Somnath Basu and Shikhar Pandey helped me with copy-editing and putting the references in order. Ashok Srinivasan provided an improvement to the title.

Pallavi and Darren encouraged me even as they made fun of odd-sounding terms like monopsonistic. My greatest debt is to Govind. She kept me going when I did not get the support I was seeking to carry out this study. For years, we have been debating the relative importance of access to knowledge and control of resources, such as land, in creating inequality. She has been part of developing the analysis in this Element, discussing various topics over early morning coffee and any time during the day. I dedicate this Element to her.

Cambridge Elements ☰

Development Economics

Series Editor-in-Chief
Kunal Sen
UNU-WIDER and University of Manchester

Kunal Sen, UNU-WIDER Director, is Editor-in-Chief of the Cambridge Elements in Development Economics series. Professor Sen has over three decades of experience in academic and applied development economics research, and has carried out extensive work on international finance, the political economy of inclusive growth, the dynamics of poverty, social exclusion, female labour force participation, and the informal sector in developing economies. His research has focused on India, East Asia, and sub-Saharan Africa.

In addition to his work as Professor of Development Economics at the University of Manchester, Kunal has been the Joint Research Director of the Effective States and Inclusive Development (ESID) Research Centre, and a Research Fellow at the Institute for Labor Economics (IZA). He has also served in advisory roles with national governments and bilateral and multilateral development agencies, including the UK's Department for International Development, Asian Development Bank, and the International Development Research Centre.

Thematic Editors
Tony Addison
University of Copenhagen and UNU-WIDER

Tony Addison is a Professor of Economics in the University of Copenhagen's Development Economics Research Group. He is also a Non-Resident Senior Research Fellow at UNU-WIDER, Helsinki, where he was previously the Chief Economist-Deputy Director. In addition, he is Professor of Development Studies at the University of Manchester. His research interests focus on the extractive industries, energy transition, and macroeconomic policy for development.

Chris Barret
Johnson College of Business, Cornell University

Chris Barrett is an agricultural and development economist at Cornell University. He is the Stephen B. and Janice G. Ashley Professor of Applied Economics and Management; and International Professor of Agriculture at the Charles H. Dyson School of Applied Economics and Management. He is also an elected Fellow of the American Association for the Advancement of Science, the Agricultural and Applied Economics Association, and the African Association of Agricultural Economists.

Carlos Gradín
University of Vigo

Carlos Gradín is a professor of applied economics at the University of Vigo. His main research interest is the study of inequalities, with special attention to those that exist between population groups (e.g., by race or sex). His publications have contributed to improving the empirical evidence in developing and developed countries, as well as globally, and to improving the available data and methods used.

Rachel M. Gisselquist

UNU-WIDER

Rachel M. Gisselquist is a Senior Research Fellow and member of the Senior Management Team of UNU-WIDER. She specializes in the comparative politics of developing countries, with particular attention to issues of inequality, ethnic and identity politics, foreign aid and state building, democracy and governance, and sub-Saharan African politics. Dr Gisselquist has edited a dozen collections in these areas, and her articles are published in a range of leading journals.

Shareen Joshi

Georgetown University

Shareen Joshi is an Associate Professor of International Development at Georgetown University's School of Foreign Service in the United States. Her research focuses on issues of inequality, human capital investment and grassroots collective action in South Asia. Her work has been published in the fields of development economics, population studies, environmental studies and gender studies.

Patricia Justino

Senior Research Fellow, UNU-WIDER and IDS – UK

Patricia Justino is a Senior Research Fellow at UNU-WIDER and Professorial Fellow at the Institute of Development Studies (IDS) (on leave). Her research focuses on the relationship between political violence, governance and development outcomes. She has published widely in the fields of development economics and political economy and is the co-founder and co-director of the Households in Conflict Network (HiCN).

Marinella Leone

University of Pavia

Marinella Leone is an assistant professor at the Department of Economics and Management, University of Pavia, Italy. She is an applied development economist. Her more recent research focuses on the study of early child development parenting programmes, on education,and gender-based violence. In previous research she investigated the short-, long-term and intergenerational impact of conflicts on health, education and domestic violence. She has published in top journals in economics and development economics.

Jukka Pirttilä

University of Helsinki and UNU-WIDER

Jukka Pirttilä is Professor of Public Economics at the University of Helsinki and VATT Institute for Economic Research. He is also a Non-Resident Senior Research Fellow at UNU-WIDER. His research focuses on tax policy, especially for developing countries. He is a co-principal investigator at the Finnish Centre of Excellence in Tax Systems Research.

Andy Sumner

King's College London and UNU-WIDER

Andy Sumner is Professor of International Development at King's College London; a Non-Resident Senior Fellow at UNU-WIDER and a Fellow of the Academy of Social Sciences. He has published extensively in the areas of poverty, inequality, and economic development.

About the Series

Cambridge Elements in Development Economics is led by UNU-WIDER in partnership with Cambridge University Press. The series publishes authoritative studies on important topics in the field covering both micro and macro aspects of development economics.

United Nations University World Institute for Development Economics Research

United Nations University World Institute for Development Economics Research (UNU-WIDER) provides economic analysis and policy advice aiming to promote sustainable and equitable development for all. The institute began operations in 1985 in Helsinki, Finland, as the first research centre of the United Nations University. Today, it is one of the world's leading development economics think tanks, working closely with a vast network of academic researchers and policy makers, mostly based in the Global South.

Cambridge Elements ≡

Development Economics

Elements in the Series

A full series listing is available at: www.cambridge.org/CEDE

Printed in the United States
by Baker & Taylor Publisher Services